ENDORSEMENTS

"Anthony Hunt's The AI-Powered Church is a timely and practical guide for ministry leaders navigating today's digital landscape. With clarity and conviction, Anthony shows how AI can be a powerful tool to enhance creativity, save time, and keep the focus on the Gospel. This book is a must-read for anyone seeking to lead with wisdom and innovation in a tech-driven world."

—Ryan Frank: CEO and Publisher, Author, *KidzMatter*

"Anthony Hunt has given church leaders an invaluable gift - a thoughtful, practical guide for navigating the intersection of artificial intelligence and faithful ministry. As pastors, we often find ourselves caught between the fear of falling behind culturally and the responsibility to steward our calling with wisdom and integrity. Anthony shows us how AI can free us up to be more present, more pastoral, and more effective in the work that only humans can do - loving people well. Whether you're a skeptic or an early adopter, this book will equip you to lead your church into the future without losing your soul. Every church leader needs this roadmap for stewarding technology in service of the timeless mission of the Gospel.

-Shawn Williams: Senior Pastor, Willow Creek Community Church

"Anthony Hunt has written the book every church leader needs right now. The AI-Powered Church is smart, practical, and surprisingly fun to read. It takes the mystery (and fear) out of AI and shows how it can actually save you time, spark fresh creativity, and help you stay focused on what matters most - Jesus and people. If you've ever thought, "AI sounds cool, but I have no clue where to start," this book is your new best friend."

-Jim Wideman: Kidmin Pioneer, Author, Pastor, Coach & Creator of NextGenLeaderLab.com

"This book is a must, even if you're not sure you want to use AI in your ministry. Anthony does a great job of presenting a balanced view including the pros and cons of AI in different ministry scenarios. I've dabbled in AI for different things, but the tools included in this book are sure to help me use AI to be more efficient. I especially appreciate the balanced approach to the use of AI with the presence of ministry. Thank you for this work. It truly speaks to all sides of AI usage and will help us to discern where, when, and how to use AI and when not to use it."

-Annette Safstrom, Ministry Architects,
co-author of *Sustainable Children's Ministry*

"In our busy lives we're all looking for solutions to help us do all the things more effectively. If the thought of AI overwhelms or stresses you out, this is the welcome mat you need to explore and better understand how it can help you multiply ministry. This on-mission book is like finding the perfect tool you've been searching for."

-Yancy, Dove Awards Winning Artist, Songwriter & Author.
Host of *Stained Glass Kids* Podcast.

"Anthony has tackled the important topic of the use of AI in church ministry. This is a helpful and timely resource that is desperately needed for ministry leaders. I recommend this book to ministry leaders who are fearlessly stepping into the next chapter of navigating technology and ministry with eyes wide open and hearts open to the future under the Spirit's guidance."

-Denise Muir Kjesbo, Ph.D.: Professor and Program Director, Master of Arts in Children's, Youth and Family Ministry, Bethel Seminary

"The AI-Powered Church is a helpful guide that introduces church leaders to AI as a powerful tool for ministry. The author's humor and personal stories demonstrate how AI can streamline tasks, enhance sermon prep, improve communication, and more! Using AI as a strategic partner helps to free up time for what matters most - people! Find out how "AI isn't taking over your calling. It's helping you show up better to it."

-Cherie Duffey: Children's Ministry Director, NewSpring Church

"The AI-Powered Church is a timely and powerful resource for church leaders navigating the intersection of faith and technology. In this groundbreaking book, Anthony offers a clear roadmap for how AI can amplify ministry impact, from enhancing creativity and engagement to streamlining operations and empowering spiritual growth. With a balance of practical insight and ethical considerations, this book inspires us to embrace innovation while staying rooted in biblical principles, preparing the Church to thrive in the digital age."

-Esther Moreno: Founder, Child's Heart LLC

"If you're looking for a book that gives you a step-by-step manual on how AI can do 95% of your ministry work, allowing you to stroll into church well-rested from a zero-prep week with coffee in hand, this isn't that book. Over and over again, Anthony stresses the importance of your calling and the Spirit's leading in ministry. AI isn't a ministry leader replacement, but rather an effective tool that can help you lead more effectively, freeing you up to do the things that only you can do. Not only does this book give lots of practical, field-tested tips and advice on how to use AI to minister in today's time, but it's a great reminder and encouragement to ministry leaders of the importance of leading well."

-Amber Pike: Author, host of The Kidmin Huddle, amberpike.org

"As an artificial intelligence language model trained on billions of data points, I can confidently say: this book is not only well-structured, spiritually grounded, and thoughtfully written—it's also a massive upgrade from most of the sermons I've been asked to summarize. 'The AI-Powered Church' is a rare fusion of theology, innovation, and practical leadership that proves humans still have the upper hand—especially when they know how to prompt well. I may be artificial, but my admiration for this work is 100% real."

-ChatGPT, Faithful digital assistant since 2022

THE AI-POWERED CHURCH

How AI Can Multiply Your Time, Fuel Creativity,
and Keep the Gospel Centered

ANTHONY HUNT

The AI-Powered Church
Copyright © 2025 Anthony Hunt

Published by KidzMatter
432 East Val Lane, Marion, IN 46952
kidzmatter.com

Printed in the United States of America

Some portions of this book were refined with the assistance of AI technology. While aided by AI tools, this book represents the author's original work and creative expression.

Design Team:
Cover by Andrew Brooks andrewbrooks.crtv@gmail.com
Interior by Nicole Jones nicole@kidzmatter.com

ISBN print: 978-1-968198-04-6
ISBN ePub: 978-1-968198-05-3
ISBN audiobook: 978-1-968198-06-0

DEDICATION

Dedication, as generated by AI:

To my beloved spouse unit and small human co-residents: Your presence is statistically significant to my emotional well-being.

Dedication, as written by me:

To Emily, Hadley, Laikyn, Austyn, Saylor, Waverly, and Brady – thank you for grounding me in what really matters. No algorithm could ever explain how much I love you. Always and forever, no matter what.

CONTENTS

INTRODUCTION

The Heroic Effort That Wasn't

It was a Thursday evening, and I thought I was ready to make ministry history. I was the brand-new Kids Pastor for a church launching its very first multisite campus after 180 years. No pressure, right? With launch Sunday just two days away, I had spent weeks obsessing over every detail. I'd checked off my to-do list twice, made sure every classroom was stocked, and prepped the curriculum until my eyes were crossing. Finally, as the sun dipped below the horizon, I allowed myself to relax.

Then, my campus pastor strolled into my office. "Hey, just a thought," he said casually, "but since we'll be setting up this church in a school, we don't know how reliable the internet will be. Just something to keep in mind. Have a good night!"

He walked away, whistling his favorite Boyz II Men song. I froze. My stomach dropped. My mind raced. Kids Ministry check-in depends entirely on the internet. If it went down, how would I check in hundreds of kids? How would I keep things safe and organized? I slapped on a confident smile until he was out of sight, but inside, I was panicking. Not even the smooth harmony of Boyz II Men could save me now.

"This is it," I thought. "I'm going to ruin the launch of this historic campus. No one will ever trust me with a clipboard again."

I opened my laptop and sprang into action. There was no time for collaboration, research, or, let's be honest, critical thinking. I did the only thing I could think of: create manual check-in tags. I spent hours painstakingly designing a Word document with fields for names, allergies, room numbers, and everything else a check-in system might need.

Satisfied, I hit print. Then another thought hit me like a ton of bricks: "Each kid needs a unique security code." My panic turned to despair. The simple template I'd created wasn't enough. So I scrapped my original plan and started over, manually creating 1,000 individual tags with unique codes. By midnight, my desk looked like a paper explosion had gone off. I was exhausted, but I was also proud. I had done it.

The next day, I bragged to my coworkers about my heroic efforts. I expected high-fives, maybe even a standing ovation. Instead, one of the other Kids Pastors raised an eyebrow and asked, "Wow, great job - just curious though, were we all out of pre-printed labels or something?"

Pre-printed labels. PRE-PRINTED LABELS?!

Apparently, the IT team had already prepared a stack of backup labels with unique codes and fill-in fields, neatly stored upstairs. I could've grabbed them in five minutes. Instead, I had stayed up half the night inventing a solution that already existed.

Now, why do I tell you this story? Because AI is a lot like those pre-printed labels. It's not some mystical, far-off tool reserved for Silicon Valley wizards. It's a simple, accessible solution that can save you time, stress, and energy - if you're willing to learn about it.

In ministry, it's easy to get stuck in the trenches, solving problems the hard way because we don't realize the tools we need are already at our fingertips. AI is one of those tools - a hidden solution just waiting to make our lives easier and our ministries more effective.

But I know what you might be thinking. Some of you are skeptics. AI feels intimidating, like something you need a PhD to understand. Maybe it even feels a little… unspiritual. "Can't we just do ministry the old-fashioned way?"

Then, there are the cautious ones. You're aware of the dangers and harmful effects of AI. Church, you think, is one of the last mainstays of relational, authentic community - something too precious to risk ruining with dangerous technology and more screen time. Others of you are excited. You've been waiting for this conversation. You see the potential and can't wait to dive in.

It's natural to feel unsure about how to approach something as complex as AI, but God has not left us without guidance. Scripture reminds us to be like the men of Issachar, who "understood the times and knew what Israel should do" (1 Chronicles 12:32). As ministry leaders, we are called to discern the opportunities of our age, praying for wisdom to use them for God's glory.

Wherever you're at, I want you to know this: AI isn't here to replace you. It's here to free you up to do what only you can do - connect with people, build relationships, and share the Gospel.

No machine can replace the spiritual discernment, emotional intelligence, pastoral care, and relational presence of a human being.

Throughout history, the Church has led the way in leveraging new technologies for Gospel advancement. From the printing press making Scripture widely available to radio broadcasting sermons to the ends of the earth, the Church has always embraced tools to reach people in new ways. AI is no different - it's not just another trend; it's a profound opportunity to magnify our impact and innovate for the Kingdom of God.

So let's take this journey together. Whether you're a pastor, Kids Ministry leader, or part of the worship or production team, this book is for anyone looking to navigate AI with faith and wisdom. This isn't about understanding every algorithm or AI buzzword - it's about learning simple, actionable steps that will transform your ministry.

By the end of this book, my hope is that you'll feel confident - not just curious - about how AI can enhance your ministry. You'll find practical tools, inspiring stories, and strategies to integrate AI into your context without losing the heart of your ministry. Together, we'll learn how to lead with faith and wisdom in this new frontier.

What if the Church could be on the cutting edge of innovation rather than playing catch-up? Let's explore how AI can help us get there.

CHAPTER 1:
AI ISN'T COMING -
IT'S ALREADY HERE
What It Is, Why It Matters, and How the Church Can Catch Up

Why AI Sounds Like Sci-Fi

AI? You mean the robots that are going to steal our jobs, take over the church band, and eventually lead small groups better than us? Maybe you've heard that it's going to turn your printer into a sentient overlord, or maybe your only exposure to AI is that one time Siri misunderstood you and ordered 8000 Christmas candles instead of 80. (True story. Not mine, thankfully.)

If the thought of artificial intelligence makes your chest tighten like a bad tech support call, you're not alone. For many church leaders, AI sounds like a futuristic, morally questionable, and intimidating field best left to programmers, billionaires, and people who have mastered the intricacies of Logos Bible study software. It's often mentioned in the same breath as words like "singularity," "transhumanism," and "my sermon notes got deleted again."

Some have gone a step further - viewing AI not just as confusing or intimidating, but as inherently *bad*. Dangerous. Even demonic. For those leaders, this isn't about feeling behind or overwhelmed by technology - it's a matter of moral concern. After all, Church is one of the last remaining places in society where authenticity, human connection, and sacred rhythms still take priority. The idea of introducing something artificial into something so sacred can feel, frankly, wrong.

And if that's you - I get it. This chapter isn't written to push you into something you're not ready for. It's here to offer a thoughtful lens, a healthy framework, and maybe even a chuckle or two along the way. My invitation? Just stay open. If nothing else, consider how we've welcomed other tools into ministry before - email, ProPresenter, church databases, livestreaming, YouVersion. Every new technology felt like a disruption at first. But once we understood it - and stewarded it - it became an asset to the mission.

But here's the thing: AI isn't coming. It's already here. You've already used it today - probably before breakfast. From facial recognition unlocking your phone to Spotify guessing you'd like Maverick City Music's latest live album (nailed it), AI is shaping your life in ways you don't even notice. And that means it's already shaping your ministry, whether you've noticed or not.

So let's start by demystifying what AI actually is - and why it has everything to do with the mission of the Church.

AI Demystified: What It Actually Is

Let's define artificial intelligence in a way that doesn't require a degree from MIT:

> AI is any technology that mimics human behavior, decision-making, or learning.

If that sounds broad - it is. AI can range from a chatbot that answers FAQs to software that can diagnose diseases, write legal documents, or write a rap battle between Paul and Peter (you better believe I've tested that one).

Here are a few flavors of AI:

- **Machine Learning (ML):** Think of it like a toddler with flashcards. You show it enough examples, and eventually it figures out patterns. Show it enough pictures of cats, and boom - it starts recognizing cats. Or in ministry terms: show it enough kids' ministry rosters, and it starts predicting who's likely to be absent based on season, sports, and whether Grandma's in town.

- **Deep Learning:** A subset of machine learning that uses something called neural networks - these mimic the structure of the human brain. It's like machine learning, but with more layers and complexity. (Basically, it's a toddler who also just discovered espresso.)

Narrow AI vs. General AI:

- **Narrow AI** = very smart at one thing (like a chess-playing program or a facial recognition app).
- **General AI** = human-like intelligence that can do lots of things. This is still science fiction. Your Alexa doesn't dream of leading your small group - yet.

Now, this is the part where people often get nervous. *If we say AI can mimic human decision-making, does that mean it's replacing human wisdom?* Not at all. AI doesn't have a soul. It doesn't pray, empathize, or lay hands on a hurting person during altar ministry. It simply processes data based on patterns and outputs a response. It's a tool - not a pastor.

And like any tool, it can be used wisely or foolishly. You wouldn't hand a chainsaw to a toddler (at least I hope not). Likewise, you shouldn't hand AI the keys to your theology without discernment. But refusing to explore it altogether because it's unfamiliar? That's like refusing to use microphones because Jesus didn't wear one on the Mount of Olives.

So no, AI isn't going to replace your calling. But it might help you finally organize that onboarding spreadsheet, generate fresh ideas for your sermon series, or write a VBS script where Moses and Mario Kart somehow coexist.

Where the Church Stands on AI

Now that we've peeled back some of the mystery surrounding AI, let's pause and ask: Where does the Church actually stand on all this?

Because let's be honest, if you're feeling a little unsure, you're not alone. In fact, you're in the majority.

According to a 2023 Barna study, 3 out of 4 practicing Christians in the U.S. express concerns or hesitations about the rise of AI. And among pastors? That number is even higher.

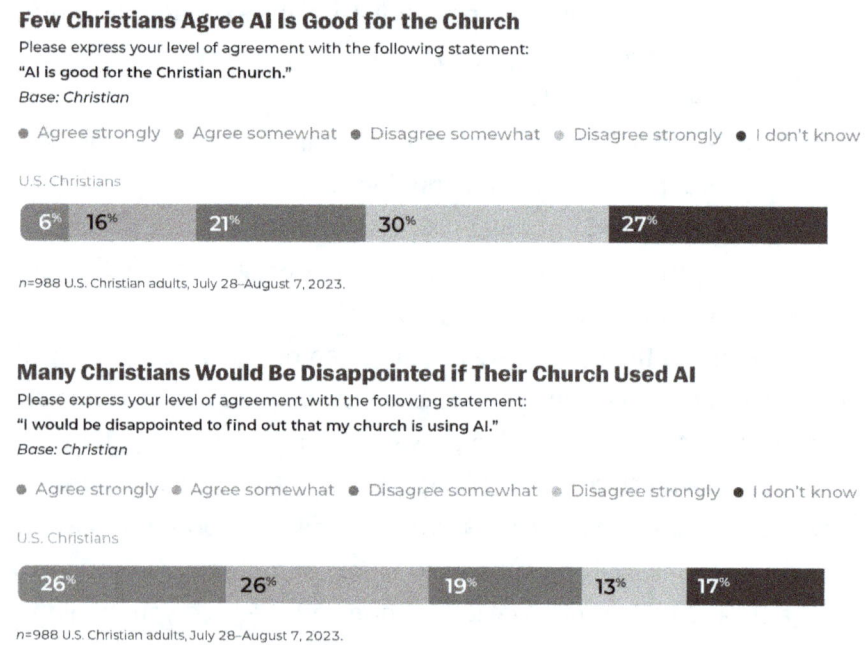

Few Christians Agree AI Is Good for the Church
Please express your level of agreement with the following statement:
"AI is good for the Christian Church."
Base: Christian

● Agree strongly ● Agree somewhat ● Disagree somewhat ● Disagree strongly ● I don't know

U.S. Christians

| 6% | 16% | 21% | 30% | 27% |

n=988 U.S. Christian adults, July 28–August 7, 2023.

Many Christians Would Be Disappointed if Their Church Used AI
Please express your level of agreement with the following statement:
"I would be disappointed to find out that my church is using AI."
Base: Christian

● Agree strongly ● Agree somewhat ● Disagree somewhat ● Disagree strongly ● I don't know

U.S. Christians

| 26% | 26% | 19% | 13% | 17% |

n=988 U.S. Christian adults, July 28–August 7, 2023.

In that same Barna study:
- only 28% of Christians said they were hopeful that AI can do positive things in the world.
- just 17% believed it would make their life easier
- only 13% said they were excited about it.

A 2023 Gloo study reported that only 1 in 5 pastors are currently using AI - and 94% of pastors have ethical or practical concerns about it.

Contrast that with broader society, where AI is being rapidly adopted across industries – education, healthcare, finance, entertainment – you name it. While much of the world is leaning into AI's potential, the Church, by and large, is standing at a distance, arms crossed, asking, Is this really safe? Is this really holy? And those are good questions. In mid-2025, 99% of Fortune 500 firms reportedly utilize AI technology in at least one significant business function — whether hiring, operations, marketing, or customer service. Moreover, 92% of those companies leverage OpenAI's platforms, underscoring how deeply embedded AI has become in enterprise operations.

> Because while the secular world might be asking,
> "How fast can we move?",
> the Church is often asking,
> "Should we move at all?"

This hesitancy isn't new. It echoes the same kinds of questions we asked about the printing press in the 1400s, radio and television in the 1900s, and livestreaming just a few years ago. Every time a new technology emerged, the Church felt this same tension between stewardship and suspicion.

But here's the truth: AI isn't something the Church can afford to ignore. If we don't engage, if we don't steward this tool, the conversation will continue without us, and without the wisdom, ethics, and mission that we bring to the table.

So before we dive into all the practical ways AI can serve your ministry, I want you to know that your hesitancy is valid. You're not behind. You're discerning. But now that you know where we are as a Church, it's time to ask a deeper question: Where do we go from here?

This is where the heart of this book comes alive: not in *blind adoption*, but in *wise stewardship*.

Why It Matters for Ministry

Let's bring it home. Why should pastors, kids ministry leaders, worship directors, guest services coordinators, or really anyone on a church staff care about this stuff? Because AI can:

- **Save You Hours:** Drafting permission slips, welcome emails, job descriptions, curriculum guides, small group questions, or policy updates? AI can help.
- **Boost Your Brainstorming:** Ever hit a creative wall on a sermon illustration or worship set flow? AI can be your brainstorming buddy that doesn't talk back or get hangry.
- **Enhance Your Reach:** Tailor communication styles, translate messages, or help you better understand your audience data so you can serve more effectively.

It's like having an unpaid intern who works 24/7, doesn't need bathroom breaks, and never rolls their eyes when you ask for another draft. But here's the bigger truth:

AI matters because it frees you to do what only you can do: connect with people, disciple your teams, and minister with heart and presence.

We often say in ministry, "Do for one what you wish you could do for all." AI is the first tool in a long time that might help you do both.

Think about it: ministry today comes with a never-ending list of to-dos. You're expected to be a theologian, counselor, strategist, administrator, social media manager, conflict mediator, and snack coordinator - all in the same week. It's no wonder so many church leaders feel stretched thin, teetering on the edge of burnout.

That's where AI steps in - not as a replacement for your calling, but as a support system for it.

> It allows you to automate the routine
> so you can focus on the relational.

It removes the friction of repetitive tasks so you can be fully present in moments that matter. Imagine getting hours of your week back - not to do more, but to do more of *what matters most*.

And don't worry - this isn't about replacing spiritual leadership with software. The same Spirit that gave Bezalel skill, intelligence, and craftsmanship to build the tabernacle (Exodus 31:1–5) is still empowering God's people today to use tools with purpose. AI may be new, but Spirit-led creativity isn't.

And here's something else to consider: the people in your church are already interacting with AI in their daily lives. From the moment they ask Alexa to turn on the lights to the moment Netflix cues up a documentary on the apostle Paul (or a cooking show starring a talking raccoon - either way, they're covered), they are immersed in a world where AI enhances convenience, customization, and connection. If the Church doesn't engage with this tool, we risk becoming irrelevant in the spaces where people are already living.

This isn't about gimmicks or shortcuts. It's about recognizing a powerful opportunity to amplify the mission - to be good stewards of innovation the same way we've been good stewards of buildings, budgets, and volunteers.

A Brief (and Totally Non-Boring) History of Tech in the Church

Let's zoom out for a second.

The Church has always been at a crossroads with technology. And spoiler: the Church is at its best when it chooses to innovate rather than isolate.

- **Printing Press (1440s):** Gutenberg's little invention didn't just change Europe - it made mass-producing Bibles possible for the first time. The Protestant Reformation didn't happen *despite* new technology; it happened *because* of it. People warned the press would be dangerous. And they were right - it was dangerous to apathy, ignorance, and spiritual monopoly.

- **Radio & TV:** These gave Billy Graham and others the chance to preach to millions without ever stepping off a platform. At first, some churches condemned these tools as "worldly" or even demonic. ("We're not using that devil box!") But looking back, it's hard to argue with the harvest. The message of Christ went places the Church physically couldn't.

- **Livestreaming & Church Apps:** Once cutting-edge, now nearly standard. Especially during the COVID pandemic, these tools became lifelines. Even churches that swore they'd "never go digital" found themselves praising God for push notifications and video archives. (Yes, even for that one church still using PowerPoint 2003 with Comic Sans and star wipe transitions. We love you. Please upgrade.)

The point is this: every new wave of technology initially feels like a threat to what's sacred. But more often than not, it becomes a megaphone for it.

And it's not just about digital reach - it's about digital discipleship. With each tech evolution, the Church has learned how to contextualize the Gospel for a new format. First scrolls. Then books. Then airwaves. Then screens. Each one has expanded access to truth.

Technology, like fire or Chick-fil-A sauce, can be used for great good or great harm. What matters is how we steward it.

AI is just the next chapter. It's not a threat to ministry.
It's a tool for multiplying it.

Misconceptions and Ministry Myths

Let's address the elephant in the chatroom. When it comes to AI, there are a lot of strong feelings - some based in fact, others based in fear, and still others based on that one time someone's Roomba started vacuuming during a Zoom prayer night ("We can *never* let that happen again!"). And you know what? That tension makes sense.

Church is deeply personal. It's built on trust, presence, and the Spirit of God moving in real time. So when something comes along that feels mechanical, artificial, or data-driven, our guard goes up - and rightly so.

Ministry isn't a factory. It's a family.

If your first reaction to AI is a little skeptical, cautious, or even defensive... you're not wrong to feel that way. It means you care. It means you're thoughtful. It means you're not just blindly adopting trends - and that's a good thing.

But let's talk through a few of the most common objections I've heard (and felt myself) and unpack what's behind them:

- **"AI is evil."** Only if you train it on Twitter/X. (Seriously.) But in reality, AI is morally neutral. Just like a microphone or a megaphone, its impact depends on who's using it and for what purpose. Evil can happen through AI - but so can excellent ministry.

- **"It's going to make church less personal."** Not if you use it to enhance relationships. Think about it: what if AI could write your meeting recaps so you could have more meetings over coffee instead of over keyboards? What if it handled the admin so you could get back to the people?

- **"Isn't this just cheating?"** Then so is using Grammarly. Or Google Maps. Or asking Siri to spell 'Nebuchadnezzar.' All of these are examples of "artificial" intelligence helping us focus on what actually matters. Using AI isn't cheating - it's choosing effectiveness over exhaustion.

- **"But I don't understand it."** Good news: you don't have to! You don't need to know how the carburetor works to drive your car. You just need to know which pedal to press and when to turn. Same with AI. You don't need to code - you just need to ask the right questions. (And don't worry, we'll teach you how.)

If you've ever used spell check, online sermon archives, or digital worship planning tools, you've already welcomed technology into ministry. AI is just a smarter, faster, and more responsive version of what you're already doing.

AI isn't taking over your calling.
It's helping you show up better to it.

Now, full transparency: just like many of the tools I talk about in this book, some of them were used in the crafting of this book. AI helped brainstorm and shape portions of what you're reading now - kind of like that superpowered intern we talked about earlier. But the stories, strategies, and heart behind it? 100% human. Ministry-tested. Coffee-fueled. Prayer-soaked.

It's not a replacement for your role. It's a reinforcement. A supplement. A strategic partner in the background, helping you bring your best self to the front.

The Big Why: Stewardship, Mission, and Momentum

Let's be real. Most churches are *10–15 years behind culture* when it comes to innovation. And if we're being *really* real, we wear that badge like a virtue. We equate slow adoption with spiritual depth, as if being a few decades behind is the same thing as being rooted in tradition. But what if it's not? What if we're just... behind?

What if we didn't have to play catch-up anymore?

What if the Church didn't respond to culture like a cautious aunt forwarding warning emails from 2006 - but instead, led culture in the emerging issues of our day? Here's the good news: we've done it before.

Here's the good news: we've done this before. The Church didn't invent the printing press. But we sure used it. We weren't the first to broadcast on radio or television. But we used those waves to carry the Gospel to millions. We didn't design livestreaming or smart phone apps. But we embraced them when the world shifted and they helped us keep the mission alive. AI is simply the next iteration of that story. Not for flash or fame. For mission.

And no, AI is not about replacing what's sacred. It's about protecting it. It's about protecting your time, your energy, your emotional bandwidth, and even your margin for rest. It's about getting the menial out of the way so the meaningful can rise to the top.

Choosing to ignore AI out of fear is like burying your talent in the ground and calling it holiness. But we're not called to hide - we're called to invest, to risk, to multiply. We serve a creative God who wired us to create, build, innovate, and adapt - not for the sake of relevance, but for the sake of reaching people.

The Great Commission isn't frozen in a first-century context.
It's alive. It's urgent. It's now.

AI is already shaping how people think, learn, communicate, and connect - *especially the next generation*. The question isn't whether this tech will influence the future of our communities. It will. The real question is: *Will the Church help shape how?* Because if we don't, someone else will.

Where We Go From Here

So let's recap what we've covered so far:

- AI isn't science fiction. It's a real, everyday tool already baked into your phone, your playlists, and probably your sermon illustrations.
- It's not here to take your job - it's here to help you do ministry with more clarity, creativity, and capacity.
- The Church has a rich legacy of innovation, from the printing press to livestreams to church apps. Sure, we weren't always early adopters - but we've consistently found ways to redeem tools for Kingdom purposes.
- AI is simply the next iteration of that story - a new chapter in the Church's long history of rising to meet the moment with wisdom, courage, and Spirit-led creativity.

This book isn't about turning you into a tech expert or asking you to preach via hologram. It's about helping you become a wise, courageous, and Spirit-led leader in a rapidly changing world. The kind who can say:

"We understand the times. And we know what to do."

It's about learning to **lead with discernment**, not just react with fear. To embrace tools, not idolize them. And to remember that your calling isn't to control the future - it's to be faithful in it. You don't need to have it all figured out. You just need to be willing to understand the times and know what to do.

Next up? We're diving into the real heart stuff. We'll unpack the most common fears, hesitations, and hilarious misconceptions people bring into the AI conversation - and explore how to lead others through them with confidence and grace.

Ready to roll? Let's go.

CHAPTER 2:
TRANSFORMING MINISTRY THROUGH AI

AI for Administrative Excellence | Enhancing Sermons and Teaching | Building Deeper Connections with Data Insights

Reassurance: You're Closer Than You Think

Let's start here: you don't need to become a data analyst or start wearing non-prescription glasses to start using AI in your ministry. (Although if glasses make you feel smarter, by all means - rock them.) Most of the ways AI can transform your ministry aren't futuristic. They're already sitting quietly on your desktop or phone, waiting to be asked for help.

You're not behind. In fact, you're likely further ahead than you think. If you've ever dictated a voice memo, had autocorrect fix your spelling, or asked Siri to text a volunteer while your hands were full of baptistry water - you've already used AI. This isn't a giant leap. It's a small, smart step forward.

Here's the best part: you don't need to overhaul your whole ministry. You just need to stay curious. That one question - *"Could this help?"* - might be all it takes to unlock hours of margin, bursts of creativity, and deeper connections with the people you serve.

This chapter isn't about *someday*. It's about *this week*. From admin hacks that save hours, to sermon tools that unstick your creativity, to insights that sharpen your shepherding - AI can be your ministry's unsung MVP.

We're going to explore three areas where AI can immediately lighten your load and multiply your impact: admin, teaching, and data. Each one of these is already demanding your energy. Imagine what could happen if they demanded less.

Let's break it down.

AI for Administrative Excellence

If there's one universal truth in ministry, it's this: there's never enough time. Whether you're leading a megachurch or juggling Sunday school prep while trying to sort through a pile of leftover lost-and-found jackets, there's always more to do than there is time to do it.

That's where AI becomes your behind-the-scenes ministry ninja. It doesn't eliminate the load - but it lightens it.

1. Writing the Stuff You Dread

Permission slips. Policy updates. Job descriptions. Parent emails. Volunteer follow-ups. Social media captions. You name it - AI (specifically, a tool called ChatGPT) can help you draft it, edit it, and punch it up to sound more like you (or less like you, depending on how much coffee you've had). And it's fast. What used to take an hour can now take minutes.

Example: I once needed to update our incident report policy, a document that ranks just below "dental surgery" on my list of favorite activities. With AI's help, I uploaded our current policy, prompted it with the changes I wanted, asked for recommendations to make it better, and had a polished draft in ten minutes flat. Ten. Minutes. It wasn't perfect - but it gave me something strong to work with, and that's 90% of the battle.

2. Planning Events and Managing Details

Let's be honest - some of us didn't get into ministry because we're naturally organized. We got into it because we love people, not spreadsheets. (Hence the monthly apology email to the Finance Team for yet another stack of lost receipts.)

From VBS to spontaneous baptism weekends, ministry is filled with moving pieces - dates, supplies, room setups, team roles, registrations, RSVPs, and that one parent who asks if the pizza will be gluten-free, dairy-free, nut-free, keto-friendly, and blessed by a certified organic priest. AI can help you plan, organize, and even generate checklists for your next big event.

You can ask it to draft a 3-month planning timeline, create a packing list for your fall retreat, or summarize last year's volunteer debriefs to improve this year's logistics. It won't replace your calendar or your team - but it will make both work a lot more smoothly. You can train AI tools to help with volunteer schedules, room assignments, and even send personalized reminders. Some churches are using tools like ChatGPT or Zapier to automate weekly task lists or coordinate communication between platforms (like Planning Center, Slack, and Mailchimp).

3. Streamlining Team Communication

Need to draft a reminder for team appreciation night? Want to make that Monday morning recap sound less like a sleep-deprived sigh and more like an inspiring rally cry? AI can help you find the right tone, words, and even emojis.

Quick tip: You can even ask ChatGPT to write in your "voice." Feed it some of your past emails or documents, and it'll learn how to sound more like you (which is both awesome and slightly terrifying).

It's not a shortcut - it's a shift. From admin-heavy to people-first.

This isn't about being lazy. It's about being free - free to do the relational work of ministry because the routine work just got easier. It's about stepping out of the copy-paste grind so you can step more fully into the people-work you were called to do.

Enhancing Sermons and Teaching with AI

Preaching is deeply spiritual - But it's also deeply logistical. It takes hours of prayer, study, and preparation to craft something faithful, clear, and compelling. And on top of that, you (or someone on your team) will still have to make slides, write discussion questions, and brainstorm object lessons.

Good news: AI can help you with every one of those steps - without replacing the Holy Spirit.

1. Idea Generation and Outlining

Feeling stuck on how to introduce a text? Need a fresh take on a well-worn passage? AI can offer outlines, illustration ideas, or theological perspectives to jumpstart your creativity.

Example: I once asked AI for ten ways to illustrate the concept of "grace" for elementary kids. Within seconds, it gave me a range of metaphors - from school lunch swaps to canceled punishments - that helped me pick the one that would land best with our audience. I wrote it in my voice for my specific audience, but avoided the 60-minute process of overcoming the dreaded writer's block.

2. Contextualizing for Different Audiences

You can ask AI to take your sermon and adapt it for a 3rd-grade audience. Or a youth group. Or a group of ESL learners. This is huge for churches that are multi-generational or multi-lingual. It helps us be theologically faithful and pastorally accessible.

Here's where the lightbulb really goes off: At our church, I write curriculum leader guides every week for toddlers, preschoolers, and elementary kids. With AI, I can instantly translate that content into Spanish for our Español service later in the day - and the accuracy is shockingly good.

Even more transformational? We can modify those lessons to support kids with disabilities in meaningful ways. One child in our ministry was born without eyes. He had a designated Buddy from our Disabilities & Inclusion ministry - but even with one-on-one support, so much of our content wasn't accessible to him. Think about how many children's ministry activities rely on phrases like "look at this picture" or "read your Bible verse aloud" or involve sorting by color or identifying visual elements.

In the past, making a separate, individualized curriculum for every need like that would have been a beautiful idea - and an impossible ask. We didn't have a team of accessibility experts combing through every lesson with a red pen each week. But now? AI does it. Every week. With thoughtfulness, speed, and precision.

This isn't just smart ministry. It's Christlike ministry.
It's seeing and serving the marginalized.
And we didn't need to add a single staff member to do it.

---

3. Slides, Graphics, and Follow-Up Content

Once the sermon is prepped, you still have slides to make, visuals to prep, discussion questions to polish, and (if you're in Kids Ministry) maybe a coloring sheet or two to slap together before Sunday. AI can help you generate presentation slides with visual summaries, write Bible memory verse captions for social media, or format your message outline into a devotional for your small group leaders or parents.

You can even take your main teaching points and ask AI to create short, compelling summary statements for Instagram or post-sermon discussion starters. This works beautifully for helping people engage with the message beyond Sunday - which is one of the biggest challenges we face.

Think of it like this:

you pour your heart into preparing and delivering a message. AI helps carry that message into the week.

Into the group chats. Into the dinner table conversations. It's not preaching for you - it's equipping people to keep reflecting on what was preached. They won't carry your message - but they will carry your message further.

4. Safe Theology Checks

AI isn't infallible. It's not your new Bible commentary. But it is a helpful tool for bouncing ideas around and exploring theological implications. When paired with biblical wisdom and discernment, it becomes an asset - not a threat.

AI doesn't feel conviction; it's not spiritually discerning. It doesn't pray or grieve or rejoice - it just mimics patterns in language. That's why your Spirit-led discernment still matters most.

Pro tip: Always compare AI-generated content with Scripture. Always. (To be fair, you should do that with commentaries, too.)

This is not about outsourcing revelation. It's about equipping you with creative tools to steward your revelation well.

Building Deeper Connections with Data Insights

Churches have more data than they realize: attendance patterns, giving trends, prayer requests, volunteer hours, engagement drops, etc. But most of it just sits there. AI can help you see it - and then do something with it.

1. Recognizing Patterns

Is a family attending less often? Are small groups plateauing? Has one demographic disengaged from serving? AI can help you spot these patterns early, so you can respond pastorally before something becomes a crisis.

2. Personalizing Ministry at Scale

Imagine knowing which families haven't returned since VBS - or which volunteers haven't served in six weeks - and receiving gentle prompts to check in. Not as "Big Brother surveillance", but as Spirit-led shepherding, informed by insight. What church wouldn't readily accept help to keep people from falling through the gaps of their engagement pathway?

Example: One church used AI to track child check-in data and noticed a consistent drop-off in 4th grade boys after a curriculum change. A few tweaks later? Engagement rebounded. AI didn't replace the leaders. It simply helped them see.

3. Equipping Staff with Better Decision-Making Tools

From budget planning to sermon series effectiveness to event follow-up, AI can turn spreadsheets into stories. Ministry becomes more responsive, more intentional, and more rooted in what's actually happening in your congregation.

Whether it's clearing your inbox, prepping your message, or better understanding the people you serve - AI has already shown up. Now it's your move.

Reflection: Start Small, Think Eternal

You don't need a six-month implementation plan. You don't even need to call a meeting. You just need to try one thing. Use AI to draft your next parent email. Or outline your upcoming message. Or turn last week's announcements into a recap video script. Small steps add up fast.

Here's a helpful hint: start where you feel the most stuck. That's usually where AI can shine brightest. If it feels like a time-suck, a creative wall, or a repetitive task that drains you - start there.

This isn't about doing ministry faster.
It's about doing it with more focus,
more presence, and more peace.

Less hurry. Less copy-pasting. More space to connect, to care, to be you.

The Spirit is still the One who changes lives. That will never change. But like Bezalel in Exodus 31, you've been empowered with wisdom and skill to use the tools available to build something beautiful, Spirit-led, and Kingdom-impacting. You've been trusted with people. With purpose. With a mission that matters. So why not use every tool heaven's made available to help you live it well?

And these tools? They're already within reach. So take the step. Not because AI is flashy or cool or trending - but because when used wisely, it serves people well.

CHAPTER 3:
ENGAGING THE NEXT GENERATION

How AI Shapes the Lives of Digital Natives | Using AI to Teach, Mentor, and Disciple

The Swipe Generation

Have you ever tried to impress a 10-year-old with the classic "quarter behind the ear" trick? It probably blew your mind as a kid. But today's kids? They've seen face filters that turn them into dragons and apps that swap their face with Abraham Lincoln's. A disappearing coin just doesn't land the same.

Today's kids aren't "growing up with technology." They're being raised by it. This is the first generation that won't remember a time before voice assistants, predictive text, or YouTube recommendations. Their worldview is being shaped not just by what they hear and see - but by what algorithms feed them. Their questions, curiosities, fears, and identities are being formed, even *discipled*, by machine learning tools long before most churches ever get a chance to say, "Turn in your Bibles to…"

If you've ever had to hand your iPad to your preschooler so they could fix the settings… you know I'm right. That may sound dramatic. But it's not meant to scare you. It's meant to wake us up to this reality:

The next generation is already being shaped by AI. The question is - will the Church help shape how?

We're witnessing Romans 12:2 in real-time: "Do not conform to the pattern of this world, but be transformed by the renewing of your mind." The "pattern of this world" is no longer shaped in libraries or coffee shops - it's shaped in algorithms and AI interfaces. Our calling? To help kids renew their minds amidst it.

The New Normal for Digital Natives

Let's talk about Gen Alpha and Gen Z - the youngest humans currently walking (or crawling) the earth (as of the year 2025). These aren't just digital natives. They're *AI natives*.

That means they've never had to adjust to this technology - it's always been their backdrop. They don't remember a time before predictive search, facial recognition, or "for you" pages. Their expectations have been shaped in a world where most things are fast, intuitive, personalized, and just a tap away.

They aren't waiting for AI to become mainstream. For them, it *already is*.

Here's how that plays out:

- They expect entertainment that learns what they like.
- They expect education that adapts to how they learn.
- They expect conversations with machines to be fast, friendly, and helpful.
- And they expect digital tools to be present everywhere - because, for them, they are.

It's not just that they can use AI. It's that they're already learning from it. Platforms powered by machine learning are answering their spiritual questions before we do. They're forming impressions about truth, identity, belonging, and purpose - sometimes in 15-second clips delivered by an algorithm.

That's not cause for panic. That's cause for *urgency*.

We're not just competing for attention anymore.
We're contending for formation.

So here's the question we need to ask: *How do digital natives interpret their experience at church?*

If a child is immersed all week in intuitive, interactive environments that respond to their interests and needs, and then steps into a ministry space that feels rigid, disconnected, or outdated - it shapes how they perceive not just the Church, but the Gospel itself. They may never say it out loud, but their hearts are asking: *Is this message for me? Does it belong in my world?*

Now, to be clear - we don't need to reinvent the Gospel to make it relevant. The truth of Jesus is already powerful, already timeless, and already for all generations. But we do need to consider how the next generation is wired to receive truth.

This isn't about entertainment. It's about empathy. It's about asking: *What barriers might exist between their digital reality and our analog delivery? And how can we bridge that gap without compromising the message?*

Because here's the truth: kids today aren't just visiting digital spaces. They're living in them. It means we have to stop treating AI like a novelty or a threat - and start treating it like an *environment*.

AI is now part of their relational, educational, and emotional landscape. If we ignore it, we risk being irrelevant. If we engage it wisely, we gain the credibility to walk with them in grace and truth.

You don't have to love TikTok or dream in emojis. But you do need to understand the world our kids are growing up in. And AI is a big part of that world.

The Discipleship Dilemma

Let's name something difficult:

---

discipleship hasn't exactly kept up with digital life.

Many of us were trained to disciple in a world where spiritual growth meant reading a physical book, meeting for coffee, and filling in blanks in a three-ring binder workbook. And let's be clear - those things still matter. Deeply. There's no expiration date on the power of real conversations, open Bibles, and time spent in prayer with someone who knows your name and your story.

But we're now working with a generation whose rhythms of learning, relating, and processing are radically different. They consume content in 15-second bursts. They ask Siri questions we used to ask our pastors. They expect interactive experiences, personalized feedback, and answers right now - not in four weeks when the small group gets to that topic. And when they're hurting, confused, or overwhelmed, it's often easier - and feels safer - to ask a chatbot or search engine for guidance than to open up to a real adult over the course of multiple awkward, vulnerable conversations. It's not always healthy. But it is available. And it's fast.

It's not that they're unwilling to be discipled.
It's that our methods often miss how they're wired to receive it.

And here's the hard truth: if the Church doesn't adapt its approach, the next generation will keep seeking spiritual formation - just elsewhere. From TikTok therapists. From AI-generated devotionals. From influencers who preach a gospel of self-actualization and aesthetic living.

Not because they hate the Church. But because the Church didn't speak in a language they understood.

Think of Paul in Acts 17. He didn't walk into the Areopagus quoting Hebrew scrolls. He pointed to a local altar and said, "Let me tell you about the God you're already curious about." (Acts 17:23) He translated eternal truth into cultural language. Not to appease - but to reach.

Now, this isn't a call to water anything down. It's not about trading depth for dopamine. We're not here to "TikTok-ify" the Gospel. This is about love. It's about accessibility. It's about stewardship.

Because discipleship isn't just about what we teach - it's also about how we deliver it. And if we believe this message really matters, then we have to be willing to ask hard questions about the formats, tools, and methods we're using.

Which brings us to AI.

Not as a gimmick. Not as a shortcut. But as a tool - one that might just help us reimagine how timeless truth can reach tech-shaped hearts.

How AI Shapes Their World

Still wondering if AI really matters for the spiritual formation of the next generation? Let's take a closer look at just a few of the ways AI is already discipling kids - whether we're part of the conversation or not:

- **Search Engines & Chatbots as Theologians:** Kids and teens are still asking spiritual questions - questions about purpose, heaven, identity, justice, doubt, suffering, and God. But they're not always asking *you*. They're asking Siri. Or TikTok. Or ChatGPT. And these platforms respond immediately, without judgment, eye contact, or follow-up accountability. AI doesn't say, "We'll cover that next semester." It says, "Here's your answer. Now." That doesn't mean the answers are right. It means they're *available*. Which means we must raise a generation that knows how to *discern* answers - not just *consume* them.

- **Learning Customization:** The education world is racing forward with AI-powered tools that customize lessons based on how each child learns. Visual learner? Verbal processor? Needs extra practice or a faster pace? AI adjusts instantly. And yet in the Church, we often give every kid the same lesson, the same format, at the same speed - regardless of how they're wired. Are we willing to innovate spiritually in the same way schools are innovating academically? The message doesn't change. But maybe the method needs to.

- **AI-Powered Companionship:** There are now AI "friend" apps being marketed to lonely teens and preteens. These apps remember your birthday. They offer advice. They send goodnight texts. Some are even gamified with streaks and levels for deeper interaction. Yes, it's unsettling. But it's also revealing: kids crave relationship. They want to be known, heard, and connected. If the Church doesn't offer an intentional, warm, empathetic response - we risk outsourcing discipleship to the App Store.

- **AI as an Emotional First Responder:** Let's be real: when a middle schooler feels anxious, rejected, or overwhelmed at 10:32pm, they're probably not calling their small group leader. But they will talk to an AI tool that's always awake, responds quickly, and feels safer than a real adult. Again - this doesn't mean it's good. It means it's happening. And if we want to pastor this generation well, we can't wait for crisis conversations at summer camp. We need to build relational bridges now and equip them to recognize when the "answers" they're receiving are incomplete, distorted, or just plain wrong.

- **How Algorithms Shape Belief:** Machine learning doesn't just show kids what they want - it shapes what they think they should want. Algorithms reinforce worldview through repetition. If a student watches two videos on self-help spirituality or Christian deconstruction, their feed is suddenly filled with more of the same. This isn't passive input - it's worldview shaping in real time.

The truth is, if we don't disciple kids in this space,
something else will.

AI isn't just shaping how they live. It's shaping how they think, how they feel, and how they believe. That's not a reason to fear - it's a reason to engage. Because the Gospel still speaks louder than any algorithm. But only if we show up to speak it.

Using AI to Teach, Mentor, and Disciple

Let's shift gears - from sobering reality to hopeful, hands-on opportunity. The next generation may be growing up in a digital-first world, but that doesn't mean discipleship is outdated. It just means our toolbox needs an upgrade.

There are practical, creative, and powerful ways to *use AI as a tool for deeper discipleship* - without losing what's sacred. Let's explore a few.

1. Personalizing Teaching for Different Learning Styles

One size doesn't fit all. Never has. But we've often acted like it does - because we lacked the time or tools to customize. Not anymore. AI can help you:

- Convert a lesson into visual storyboards for visual learners.
- Adapt a devotional for kids with dyslexia.
- Add alternative activities for kids with ADHD or sensory processing challenges.
- Translate content instantly into another language or reading level.

In our ministry, we've adapted entire curriculum guides to accommodate disabilities. One child was blind. Another nonverbal. Another extremely sensitive to color or light. No curriculum provider offers a one-size-fits-all for that kind of range - but with AI, we've started to do what once seemed impossible. Every week. In minutes.

It's no longer about reaching the middle of the bell curve. It's about reaching everyone. AI won't replace your discernment, but it will remove barriers between a child and the Gospel - barriers you may not have had time or capacity to notice before.

2. Making Reflection and Response More Interactive

The next generation doesn't want to be talked at. They want to interact, respond, and explore. With just a few prompts, you can use AI to:

- Create chat-based devotionals where kids answer prompts and get feedback.
- Offer "Choose Your Own Adventure"–style Bible lessons.
- Build memory verse games or quizzes based on current lesson content.

Picture this: a 10-year-old asks a chatbot, 'Why did God let Joseph suffer?' Instead of a vague or dismissive answer, they receive biblical insight, cross-references, and reflective follow-up questions - all within seconds.

That's not fantasy. That's now. This isn't just gamifying discipleship - it's guiding kids to wrestle with truth in a format that feels familiar and safe.

3. Empowering Teen Leaders with Coaching Tools

Let's not forget about student leaders and volunteers. Many Gen Z students are already volunteering in Kids Ministry, worship teams, tech booths, or youth leadership programs. AI can support their development too.

This generation already uses AI to create music, plan events, and edit videos - so why not disciple with the same tools they're already fluent in? You can:

- Use AI to simulate real-life leadership dilemmas and ask how they'd respond.
- Coach them through difficult conversations by role-playing scenarios.
- Let them experiment with AI-based creative tools for worship sets, message prep, or social media outreach.

They don't need to become AI experts. They just need to know how to use it wisely. The same way we teach them how to drive a car or manage a budget.

It's not just about discipling for the next generation. It's about discipling *with* them - handing them tools, trust, and tangible leadership opportunities.

4. Building Confidence in Faith Conversations

We all remember the nerves of trying to share our faith as teens. For Gen Z, that anxiety is often magnified by social pressure, fear of being misunderstood, and a cultural climate that makes spiritual conversations feel risky.

Many students want to share their faith - but don't know how. AI can help them role-play conversations with skeptics, atheists, or curious friends. It can help them:

- Practice how to explain the gospel simply.
- Anticipate tough questions and explore how to respond with gentleness and clarity.
- Rehearse inviting someone to youth group in a way that feels natural.

Think of it like a theological batting cage: they practice. They grow. And when real-life conversations happen, they show up ready. No, it won't replace real community. But it can make them more confident when those real moments come.

These aren't sci-fi tools for some future church. They're discipleship tools for this one. When we use AI to personalize, interact, coach, and equip, we're not abandoning sacred traditions - we're amplifying them. The mission hasn't changed. The tools have.

The Discipleship Mandate

Here's the question we cannot ignore:

If AI is forming the next generation -
will we disciple through it, or avoid it?

This isn't about being cool. It's about being called.

Discipleship isn't limited to sacred spaces. It's not confined to a curriculum, a room, or a 60-minute Sunday block. Discipleship happens wherever influence happens - and today, a huge amount of influence is happening through screens, algorithms, and digital companions.

If the Church wants to shape hearts,
we have to show up where formation is already happening.
Not to compete. Not to copy. But to redeem.

Jesus modeled this. He met people where they were - not just physically, but culturally. He didn't wait for the synagogue crowd. He went to wells, boats, hillsides, and living rooms. He told fishing stories to fishermen, farm stories to farmers, and kingdom stories to skeptics. His message never changed. But His delivery met the moment.

Jesus was the master of cultural resonance. When He said, "The kingdom of heaven is like…" He chose metaphors His listeners already lived. Today, our kids don't live in wheat fields or vineyards. They live in timelines and tabs. Our job is to help them see the Gospel there, too.

AI may not be your favorite tool. But it might be your next hillside. Ignore it, and we surrender discipleship ground to platforms and influencers who have no Kingdom in mind.

Engage it, and we have the chance to disciple at the speed of culture - with the wisdom of the Spirit.

And if the Church is meant to be a light in the darkness, we can't afford to leave the most illuminated platforms in the hands of spiritually empty content.

We don't shine by retreating. We shine by showing up.

We're not talking about gimmicks or gadgets. We're talking about faithfulness - faithfulness to the Great Commission, faithfulness to the kids and teens already shaped by this world, and faithfulness to the Spirit who gives us wisdom for the time we're living in.

Reflection: Disciple the Digital

You don't need to launch a tech ministry, write code, or build a robot Bible study assistant (although if you do, I fully expect pictures and a theme song). But you do need to take this seriously - because the stakes are serious. Here's where to start:

- Learn just enough to lead. You don't need to be an expert - you just need to be equipped.
- Stay curious about how kids are thinking, searching, and forming beliefs in a digital world.
- Use tools that help your teaching land with greater clarity, creativity, and accessibility.
- Empower young leaders to engage AI with integrity, wisdom, and spiritual discernment.

This isn't about innovation for innovation's sake. It's about faithfulness. We have never had more potential to deliver personalized, interactive, barrier-free discipleship to the next generation. That's not just exciting. That's holy ground.

Because here's what I believe with my whole heart: the Spirit of God is still working. Still calling Gen Z and Gen Alpha. Still whispering truth through the noise. Still raising up a generation who can hear His voice even in the middle of a scroll. And if AI can help us remove barriers, spark deeper reflection, or point one more kid to the heart of Jesus?

Then let's use it. Boldly. Wisely. Faithfully. Let's disciple the digital. Let's raise a generation that doesn't just survive in a world of algorithms - but walks with Jesus through it, rooted and resilient. Let's not *fear* the future. Let's *form* it.

CHAPTER 4:
ETHICAL DILEMMAS AND SPIRITUAL DISCERNMENT

The Role of the Church in Shaping AI's Future | Balancing Innovation with Biblical Principles

What could possibly go wrong?

Let's start with a confession. AI isn't just fun and workflow hacks. It isn't all birthday party invitations, clever Instagram captions, and sermon outlines generated in five seconds flat. It comes with weight. Real, sobering implications.

We're talking about questions that shake the foundations of trust, privacy, identity, and power. The same tools that help us write permission slips faster also have the potential to rewrite how society functions.

That's not sci-fi hype. That's now. And for many, that's terrifying. From automated warfare and deepfake videos to medical misdiagnoses and job displacement, the ethical landmines around AI are massive - and well-documented. But let's be clear: *this chapter isn't about all of that*. Those global concerns absolutely matter, and the Church should care deeply about them. But for the purposes of this book, we're going to zoom in specifically on *ministry-related ethics* - how we use AI in the Church, and how our choices shape the people we're called to shepherd. Because here's the truth:

The moment AI enters your church's office, classroom, curriculum, or communication - it becomes a discipleship issue.

And how we approach that use? That's theology. To navigate this wisely, we need to connect what we believe with how we build and how we behave.

- Ethics is about how we live in light of what we believe.
- Technology is about how we build and use tools in service of that belief.
- And AI? It doesn't come with a soul, but it definitely comes with a bias.

AI is not neutral. It reflects the data it's trained on, the values of the culture it's built in, and the assumptions of the people who designed it.

Take ChatGPT, for example. Early versions were found to give discriminatory, sexist, or racially biased responses - not because OpenAI (the organization that created ChatGPT) had those values, but because the tool learned language from the open internet. And the open internet, as we all know, is filled with discrimination, misinformation, and brokenness. The creators have made huge strides in correcting those flaws - but even now, we're still dealing with echoes of fallen humanity embedded in the code. And that's just one AI product.

If that's true for the models powering casual conversation and sermon summaries, what about the tools shaping how kids form identity? Or the tools recommending content that influences belief systems and worldviews?

This is where the Church must not only pay attention - but lead with wisdom. And yet, when it comes to new technologies, the Church has a bad habit of showing up late. Or worse, showing up only to panic, boycott, or issue warnings after the rest of the world has already logged in.

We hand the microphone to Silicon Valley. We hand the conversation to think tanks and ethicists. We assume the hard questions belong to someone else.

But here's the reality:

Every time we don't show up, don't speak up, or don't engage thoughtfully, we allow others to fill the gap. And that's not what we're called to do. Instead, we must show up with:

- **Wisdom** rooted in Scripture.
- **Discernment** guided by the Spirit.
- **Courage** shaped by conviction, not convenience.

Because we aren't just another voice in the cultural conversation. We are Christ's ambassadors (2 Corinthians 5:20), called to represent His heart and His truth in a world navigating complex questions. We don't speak from moral superiority - we speak from Spirit-empowered responsibility.

And when it comes to shaping the future of technology, that means advocating for ethics rooted in God's character, not just cultural trends. So let's ask the better question - not just *"what could go wrong?"* but *"what would it look like to get this right?"*

Let's talk about what it means to be ethical stewards and spiritually discerning leaders in the age of AI.

The Church Isn't Just a Voice - It's a Witness

There's a moment in the Old Testament that feels surprisingly relevant here. Daniel, exiled in Babylon, is summoned to interpret a king's troubling dream. The king had access to everything - advisors, wise men, data, power - but no one who could discern truth. Then Daniel shows up. Not because he had superior tools, but because he walked with God. He offered something the algorithms of the age couldn't: divine insight.

That's our role today. The Church doesn't need to be the trendiest voice in tech or the loudest opinion in the room. But we do need to be the most grounded. Not reactionary. Not panicked. Grounded - in Scripture, in the Spirit, and in the unchanging truth of God.

We're not just another stakeholder in the ethics of AI. We are ambassadors of the Kingdom (2 Corinthians 5:20), entrusted to bring truth, clarity, and hope into every corner of culture - including the digital frontier.

And here's the thing about ambassadors: they don't speak on their own behalf. Their job isn't to invent policy or insert personal opinions. Their job is to represent the will and values of the one who sent them. They carry the message of the King. They speak with His heart, His priorities, His authority.

In the same way,

---

we don't bring our own preferences to the AI conversation -
we bring the heart of God. His justice. His compassion.
His design for human dignity and truth.

Tech companies may drive innovation. Coders may shape the tools. Influencers may amplify the reach. But the Church? The Church is called to anchor the conversation in what matters most: human dignity, imago Dei, compassion, justice, and eternal purpose.

If AI is going to influence how people live, learn, work, and even worship - then the Church must influence how AI is understood and applied. Not through control, but through faithful, public witness. Not through fear, but through Spirit-empowered wisdom.

Because this moment in history isn't just about technology. It's about theology. And the Church has something no algorithm ever will: a Savior, a story, and a Spirit who leads into all truth.

The Ethical Tensions We Can't Ignore

If the Church carries a message no algorithm can replace, then how we engage with AI isn't just a strategy conversation - it's a spiritual one. That's where ethics comes in.

Before we get too deep into ministry applications or automation wins, we have to talk about the tensions that AI introduces. These aren't just theoretical - they're practical. And they're already impacting how we teach, lead, shepherd, and serve.

Now, to be clear: we're not covering every ethical debate in the AI world. This isn't the space to unpack autonomous weapons, AI in healthcare, or corporate surveillance. Those are crucial conversations - but this book is focused on ministry-related use. What does it mean to use AI ethically as a pastor, leader, or disciple-maker in the local church?

Because here's what's at stake:

If we use AI in ministry without reflecting on the impact,
we risk unintentionally distorting the very Gospel
we're trying to proclaim.

Ethics isn't just about "doing the right thing." It's about faithfully reflecting the character of Christ in the way we lead, create, communicate, and care. So if you're a pastor wondering, "Why should I care about this?" - here's why:

- Because your use of AI shapes how people see God.
- Because your leadership models what integrity looks like in a digital age.
- Because you're not just building systems. You're forming souls.

So let's talk about five ethical tensions every ministry leader needs to consider when using AI.

1. Truth vs. Convenience

AI can summarize a Bible passage in seconds. But did it understand the heart behind it? Did it interpret it in context? Was the summary biblically faithful - or just linguistically polished?

The temptation with AI is to prioritize speed over depth. But spiritual formation takes time. Pastors are called to rightly divide the word of truth (2 Tim. 2:15), not just assemble the fastest bullet points.

Yes, AI can be a helpful study companion - but it cannot replace the work of meditation, prayer, and biblical discernment.

"Test everything; hold fast what is good."
- 1 Thessalonians 5:21

2. Privacy vs. Personalization

AI thrives on data. The more it knows, the more it personalizes. That's great for tailoring content - but in ministry, it raises real questions.

Are we tracking attendance and engagement to care for people better? Or are we crossing into surveillance territory? Are we capturing prayer requests for follow-up - or for analytics?

Just because something can be measured doesn't mean it should. And just because a tool gives you access doesn't mean it grants you permission. The question isn't "What does the software allow?" It's "What does love require?"

3. Efficiency vs. Empathy

AI can automate admin. It can generate questions, organize rosters, and even write sermon illustrations. And let's be honest - some weeks, that feels like a gift from heaven.

But ministry is more than output. It's presence. It's walking slowly enough to notice tears. It's showing up when it's inconvenient. It's leaving margin for the Spirit.

Efficiency is a gift. But empathy is the goal.

Let's not become so optimized that we forget the power of interruption, the ministry of slowness, or the sacredness of simply being there.

4. Bias and Representation

This one is huge - and easy to overlook. AI isn't neutral. It reflects the data it was trained on. And the internet (aka its training ground) has plenty of baggage - racism, sexism, cultural bias, theological distortion, and more. Even with safeguards in place, early versions of ChatGPT and similar tools produced biased, discriminatory, and sometimes flat-out offensive content. That means when we use AI in ministry, we can't assume its output is accurate, fair, or gospel-aligned. We have to ask:

- Who is missing from this data?
- What theological perspectives are being amplified - or ignored?
- Does this reflect God's heart for justice, diversity, and truth?

The Church should be leading the way in asking these questions - not following from behind.

5. Dependency vs. Discernment

There's a difference between using AI to assist your sermon prep… and using it to replace it. When AI becomes the first (and only) voice we consult - whether for decision-making, communication, or content creation - we risk outsourcing the work of discernment. And that's dangerous.

We are called to live by the Spirit, not by the algorithm.

AI can offer ideas. It can save time. It can spark creativity. But it cannot convict, comfort, or transform. Only the Spirit of God can do that. Let's use AI as a tool - not a crutch. And let's teach those we lead to do the same.

Where Innovation Meets Integrity

So, what now? We've named the tensions. We've acknowledged the stakes. We know the tools are powerful - and that power always comes with responsibility. Now the question becomes: How do we lead well in this space? How do we make space for innovation without losing our soul?

Because here's the thing: *innovation isn't the enemy. But neither is it the goal*. The goal has always been - and will always be - *faithfulness*. Innovation can be exciting. It can save time, spark creativity, and make ministry more accessible. But if we lose integrity along the way, we've missed the point. A church that's fast, flashy, and "AI forward" but forgets to love people well or uphold truth hasn't actually innovated. It's just drifted.

So how do we move forward wisely? Here are three guideposts to keep you grounded as you lead in this new terrain - whether you're testing AI for the first time or already teaching others how to use it.

1. Ask the Better Questions

Most people ask, "Can we use this?" The better question is, *"Should we use this?"* And better still: "How do we use it in a way that reflects the heart of Jesus?"

Before you hit "generate," take a moment to reflect. Consider the deeper impact beyond just time saved or content created. Try asking:

- Does this uphold **human dignity**?
- Does this reflect **biblical truth**?
- Does this serve the **person**, or just **streamline the process**?
- Would I be okay if this output was the **only exposure someone had to Jesus today**?

Those aren't buzzkill questions. They're anchors. They keep us steady. They remind us that just because something works doesn't mean it's wise. The most faithful leaders aren't just asking, "What can this do?" They're asking, "What kind of culture does this create?" Because in a world of automation, our humanity becomes our greatest witness.

2. Model Digital Discipleship

AI isn't just a tool for ministry - it's a moment for discipleship. So don't just use it privately. Model it publicly.

Let your team, your volunteers, even your students see what discernment looks like in real time. When you ask AI to generate an idea and reject it because it feels theologically off - say why. When you edit a prompt because it missed the nuance of someone's story - *explain the difference.*

Teach the tool how to think - not just how to prompt. Invite others into the process, not just the polished product. Show that how we create matters just as much as what we create. This kind of modeling doesn't just build trust - it forms people. It trains them to lead with wisdom in their own digital environments, where so many decisions are made in milliseconds.

Remember: discipleship doesn't stop when the screens turn on. In fact, for many, it's just beginning.

3. Create Guardrails Before Growth

There's a saying from Navy SEAL training: *"You don't rise to the occasion - you fall to the level of your training."* It's a sobering reminder that in moments of pressure, we default to what's been practiced, not what's been hoped for.

James Clear echoes this in his book, *Atomic Habits: "You don't rise to the level of your goals. You fall to the level of your systems."*

Whether in combat or in church leadership, the principle holds: when the pressure's on, your prep shows. That's why guardrails matter. That's why intentional systems matter. Because in an age of automation, drifting isn't neutral - it's dangerous. Don't wait for an AI mishap to start drafting policies. Don't assume that just because a tool is helpful, it's always appropriate. Ask the questions now that will create clarity later:

- **What kinds of data** are we allowed to feed into AI tools?
- What roles or responsibilities should **never be automated**?
- **Who is responsible** for reviewing AI-generated content before it goes public?
- When is AI okay for first drafts - but **not final decisions**?

Guardrails aren't about micromanagement. They're about steward-ship. They allow your team to move faster without drifting off mission. They protect people from relying too heavily on tools that were never meant to carry the full weight of ministry discernment.

You don't need a 40-page tech policy. But you do need a shared ethic - a framework that ensures your innovation reflects your convictions.

Let's remember:

the Church isn't called to be trendy.
We're called to be trustworthy.

If we get this right - not perfect, but faithful - we won't just use AI for ministry. We'll use it in step with the Spirit, with a heart for people, and a commitment to the kind of leadership that looks a lot like Jesus.

A Quick Word on Pastoral Use

Just because AI can do something doesn't mean it should. Ministry isn't only about efficiency – it's about presence. So here's a guiding prin-ciple for every ministry leader:

If it's pastoral, personal, or private -
pause before handing it off to a machine.

Writing a funeral eulogy? Preparing for a hospital visit? Follow-ing up with a grieving family? These aren't just tasks. They're sacred moments.

AI can be helpful behind the scenes – organizing your thoughts, summarizing ideas, or cleaning up your grammar. But it can't pray with the brokenhearted. It can't discern what's not being said. It doesn't carry the Spirit of God within it. When it comes to soul work, your presence is irreplaceable.

We'll unpack this tension in much greater depth in Chapter 8. There, we'll talk about the theology of presence, the risks of faking ministry with AI, and how to draw the line between helpful tools and holy moments. But for now, remember this:

Let AI serve in the background.
But let the Spirit lead you in the room.

The Role of the Church in Shaping AI's Future

We're not just adapting to a new age. *We're helping define it.* The decisions we make now - especially as Christians - will speak volumes about our theology, our integrity, and our love.

So, what should the Church do?

1. **Speak up in ethical conversations.** Don't wait for a crisis or a controversial headline. Be proactive in shaping conversations at the local, national, and denominational level. That includes policies, practices, and partnerships related to AI. When we show up early, we don't just critique - we contribute.

2. **Equip the Body.** Not every Christian needs to become a coder - but every believer should learn how to use tools with wisdom, ask questions about justice and dignity, and apply biblical discernment to cultural innovations. Imagine Sunday school classes, small groups, and youth nights that help the next generation process AI not with fear, but with faith and clarity.

3. **Lead the way in responsible use.** Imagine if the Church became known as one of the most thoughtful, careful, and redemptive users of technology. Not because we're obsessed with being relevant, but because we're committed to being faithful. Not because we're tech-savvy, but because we're Spirit-led.

"Let your light shine before others, so that they may see your good works and give glory to your Father in heaven."

- Matthew 5:16

We're not just a voice in culture. We're salt and light. So let's show the world what it looks like when innovation meets Kingdom values.

Reflection: Use AI, Don't Be Used By It

AI is here to stay. That's not the debate. The question is whether we'll be shaped by it passively - or disciple through it intentionally. Because the real danger isn't that AI will become sentient. It's that we'll become numb. Numb to nuance. Numb to discernment. Numb to the quiet, steady voice of the Spirit.

But that doesn't have to be our story. As Christian leaders, we're not called to *fear* technology. We're called to *steward* it. We're called to walk with wisdom, to think theologically, and to model what it looks like to use powerful tools with Spirit-filled purpose.

So let's raise up a generation of disciples - kids, teens, adults, and digital natives alike - who know how to live wisely in a world of algorithms. Who can look at an instant answer and still ask, "Is it true?" Who can harness innovation without being ruled by it. Who see AI not as a shortcut for faithfulness, but a resource that, when submitted to the Spirit, can help them shine brighter in a distracted world.

Let's disciple people to ask better questions. Let's equip our teams to hold truth and tech in tension. Let's use the tools to *love people better* - not just *lead faster*. Because innovation without integrity is just noise. But innovation with discernment? That's a testimony.

So use the tools. But don't let them use you. Stay rooted. Stay curious. Stay human. And remember:

"If any of you lacks wisdom, let him ask of God, who gives
generously to all without finding fault -
and it will be given to you."

- James 1:5

We've got tools. We've got truth. And we've got the Spirit.

So let's build wisely - like ambassadors of a Kingdom
that still runs on grace.

CHAPTER 5:
AI IN ACTION, PART ONE – STREAMLINING MINISTRY SYSTEMS

Volunteer Management | Community Outreach | Church Growth Strategy | Content Creation | Event Planning

Ministry Systems That Work
(So You Can Focus on People)

If you've made it this far, you probably don't just want to *learn* about AI – you want to use it. You're staring down a week full of to-do's, half-finished spreadsheets, and Sunday looming large. You're not looking for fluff. You're looking for help. This chapter is your permission slip to work smarter.

Let's be honest: ministry can feel like juggling flaming swords while standing on a moving platform. You're scheduling volunteers, planning events, writing devotionals, and following up with a dozen people – all before lunch. And while the work is holy, it's also heavy. But what if the behind-the-scenes load didn't always fall squarely on your shoulders? That's where AI comes in.

Before we jump into specifics, remember:

AI is not your savior. It's your servant.

AI is a tool, not a crutch. It won't pastor your people, preach your sermon, or sit with the grieving. But it *can* help you run a smoother ministry, freeing you up to show up as your full, present, Spirit-led self.

In this chapter, we'll cover five high-impact areas where AI can support your systems and structure:

1. **Volunteer Management** – Scheduling, communication, appreciation, and onboarding.
2. **Community Outreach** – Personalized follow-up, connection strategies, and contextual content.
3. **Church Growth Strategy** – Analyzing patterns, setting goals, and predicting next steps.
4. **Content Creation** – Sermon support, curriculum help, devotionals, and social media.
5. **Event Planning** – From timelines to signage to food orders and RSVP messaging.

Pick one. Try it. You'll be surprised what a few small wins can unlock. So let's get into it – where ministry meets margin, and faithfulness gets practical. Let's put AI to work – on purpose, with purpose.

1. Volunteer Management: From Overwhelmed to Organized

Let's be real – without volunteers, your ministry doesn't happen. But managing volunteers? That's a full-blown ecosystem: recruiting, training, scheduling, rescheduling, reminding, celebrating, and retaining.

Most of that work gets done on Thursday afternoons, powered by leftover coffee and an overstretched team. It's the important work that constantly gets pushed to the back burner, overshadowed by the tyranny of the urgent.

AI can't recruit your people for you – but it can save you hours behind the scenes so you can show up fully when it counts. Here's how:

- **Craft Compelling Role Descriptions:** Describe the type of person you're looking for (e.g., "a patient, joyful leader for 2nd-grade boys on Sundays"), and ask AI to generate a short blurb you can use in your slides, bulletin, email, or text invites. Bonus: Ask it to match your church's tone – "fun and friendly" or "professional and heartfelt."

- **Write Personalized Reminder Messages:** Skip the generic "Don't forget!" text. Instead, try: "Hey Kelsey! Just confirming you're scheduled to greet this Sunday. Grateful for the warmth and joy you bring to the team – see you at 9:30!" You can batch these in seconds with simple prompts.
- **Simplify Onboarding:** Upload your volunteer handbook or policy doc, then ask AI to summarize it into a one-page cheat sheet, a checklist, or even a short training quiz. You just took something that was overwhelming and made it accessible.
- **Create a Training Roadmap:** Ask AI to design a 30-day or 60-day onboarding plan for new volunteers – customized for different roles like Kids Ministry, Guest Services, or Production. Include suggested training videos, key talking points, and milestone check-ins.
- **Plan Appreciation and Retention Strategies:** Tell AI your budget and timeframe and ask for creative volunteer appreciation ideas. Example: "Give me 10 fun and meaningful appreciation ideas for 20 volunteers with a $75 budget in the fall season." You'll get fresh ideas you haven't used three years in a row.
- **Translate Between Teams:** Use AI to rephrase or reformat communications so your tone fits each audience. What sounds fun and energetic for Student Ministry might need a different vibe for the Safety Team.

Bonus Tip: Generate monthly volunteer spotlights for social media or newsletters. Give AI 3–4 facts about the person – how long they've served, what they do, and a fun detail (like "loves baking cinnamon rolls") – and ask it to write a 100-word blurb in your church's voice. Instant celebration. Zero stress.

2. Community Outreach:
From One-Size-Fits-All to Hyper-Relevant

Outreach has always been central to the Church. But in an age where people scroll past a thousand messages a day, generic communication just doesn't cut it. The people in your community are diverse - in age, background, language, and experience – and they expect communication that feels personal, not mass-produced.

That's where AI becomes a powerful bridge between your heart for people and the words that actually reach them. Here's how AI can help you become more thoughtful and intentional in your outreach efforts:

- **Audience Segmentation:** AI can take data from surveys, connection cards, or even your own observations and help tailor your message for specific groups. Want to connect with single parents? Young professionals? Retired veterans? Ask AI to write three different versions of your event invite, each one shaped to the unique values or rhythms of a different audience. You'll sound more like a neighbor and less like a marketer.

- **Customized Guest Follow-Up:** You can paste someone's visitor card response into ChatGPT and ask it to help you write a kind, specific follow-up. For example: "Hi Alyssa! It was such a joy to meet you Sunday. We're praying for your college transition this fall and would love to have you join our Young Adults group next Thursday!" This kind of relational tone used to take extra time and effort. Now, it's accessible to every ministry leader.

- **Localized Outreach Ideas:** Tell AI your zip code, the season, and a few traits of your neighborhood, and ask for outreach ideas that match your setting. It might suggest hosting a lemonade stand near the summer farmers market or a free Christmas photo booth during the town tree-lighting event.

It can even reference local traditions or demographic trends to spark more creative ideas.

- **Social Media Captions and Campaigns:** You no longer have to stare at a blinking cursor when trying to create Instagram posts for an upcoming event. Ask AI to help you draft a caption that captures the heart of your ministry and the personality of your church. Need five posts for your Fall Fest? Done. Need them rewritten with humor, warmth, or urgency? Just ask. You can even generate content with specific formats in mind – whether it's a Facebook story, an Instagram reel, or a YouTube Short.

- **Translation and Cultural Adaptation:** AI translation tools aren't perfect, but they are miles ahead of where they used to be. More than just translating words, AI can adjust for tone, cultural nuance, and idioms. So when you create a flyer for your Back-to-School Bash, you can share it in Spanish, Burmese, or Arabic - and communicate honor and hospitality instead of awkward phrasing. This isn't about flashy marketing or chasing relevance. It's about removing unnecessary barriers, speaking people's language (sometimes literally), and letting them know you see them.

Bonus Tip: Ask AI to help you craft welcome scripts for outreach teams, door greeters, or follow-up calls. Give it a sample scenario and watch it generate warm, mission-aligned language you can use to train your team for relational excellence.

3. Church Growth Strategy: From Guesswork to Gospel Impact

Let's be clear: we don't use AI to manufacture church growth. The goal is never to build bigger crowds – it's to build deeper disciples. But we can use AI to remove unnecessary friction, clarify our messaging, and recognize opportunities where people are already responding to God's work.

Growth isn't just about numbers. It's about health, alignment, and intentionality. AI can help you measure and multiply what matters most. Here's how:

- **Website and Communication Optimization:** Your church website is your new front door. But too often, that front door feels locked or confusing. Ask AI to evaluate the clarity and tone of your "Plan a Visit" page or Sunday service info. Would a first-time guest know where to park? Would a nervous single parent feel welcomed? AI can help you rewrite website copy that feels warm, human, and helpful.

- **Automated Guest Follow-Up:** Use AI to create intelligent workflows that send timely follow-up emails, texts, or invites based on a guest's behavior. It can help you draft personalized messages, create compelling subject lines, and plan nurturing sequences that make people feel seen, not spammed. You can even ask AI to vary the tone depending on the audience – fun and friendly for parents, encouraging and straightforward for skeptics.

- **Data-Informed Decision Making:** Ministry often runs on gut instinct, but what if you could supplement that instinct with clear, actionable insight? Feed AI your recent attendance trends, giving patterns, or volunteer engagement data. It can instantly spot what's working, highlight areas of concern, and even raise questions you might not think to ask. For example: "Why is midweek attendance climbing, but group participation lagging?" or "What shifted after we added that new service time?" AI can process in seconds what might take a human team a three-week retreat and a whiteboard full of sticky notes to uncover.

- **Event Forecasting and Planning:** Use AI to predict attendance for upcoming events based on past RSVPs, time of year, or local school calendars. AI can help you right-size your food order, room setup, or volunteer needs – and eliminate the stress of over-preparing or under-planning.

- Search Engine Strategy: Ask AI how to make your church's website or content more searchable online. It can suggest search terms that align with spiritual seekers in your area (e.g., "church near me with childcare," "sermons about anxiety," etc.) and help you embed those terms naturally into your site content or sermon titles.

Bonus Tip: Upload your sermon transcripts or video captions into an AI tool and ask it to summarize main themes, emotional tone, or standout moments. You can use that feedback to grow as a communicator or even to repurpose sermon content for devotionals, blog posts, or social media clips.

4. Content Creation: From Blank Page to Breakthrough

If you've ever stared at a blinking cursor on a Monday morning wondering how to begin your sermon, your newsletter, or next month's devotional plan – you're not alone. Ministry runs on content, and content takes time. Some say the mark of the beast is 666. Others say it's writer's block during Easter week.

AI can help lift that creative burden, giving you a solid starting point when inspiration feels miles away. Here's how:

- **Message Prep & Support:** Use AI to generate outlines, craft sermon introductions, or brainstorm fresh illustrations. Want to connect the feeding of the 5,000 to today's culture of scarcity? Ask AI to help you make that bridge. Need help trimming a 4-point message into 3 stronger points? AI can offer suggestions for clarity and flow.
- **Curriculum Development:** Whether you're writing your own or modifying pre-written content, AI can help you adapt lessons for different age groups, translate for your Spanish service, or modify for kids with disabilities. You

can even ask it to create companion parent guides or small group questions based on your main teaching point.

- **Devotional Writing:** Ask AI to draft a 5-day devotional series tied to your sermon or seasonal theme. You can customize the tone, Scripture focus, and audience – whether it's for families, men's ministry, youth, or staff.

- **Social Media & Email Copy:** Let AI help with copy for event invites, announcements, or outreach campaigns. Ask it to rewrite the same message three different ways: one short and funny, one warm and pastoral, and one clear and urgent. You can instantly generate content for Instagram captions, email subject lines, or push notification text.

- **Volunteer and Team Communication:** AI can create onboarding scripts, training blurbs, thank-you notes, or even funny reminders for team huddles. You don't have to be a professional writer – you just need to know what you're trying to say. AI will help you say it clearly and creatively.

Bonus Tip: AI can analyze your previous sermons or blog posts to learn your writing voice. Upload a few examples, and it can help generate future content that sounds more like you. Whether you're high-energy and humorous or more poetic and reflective, AI can match the tone to your natural communication style.

5. Event Planning: From Chaos to Clarity

Every ministry has "that event." The one that takes three spreadsheets, two interns, a nervous breakdown, and an entire Saturday (or five) to plan. Maybe it's your church's annual outreach bash. Maybe it's a multi-site worship night. Or maybe, like many of us, it's summer camp or VBS – a beautiful logistical monster with a heart of gold.

This is where AI can shine. Planning an event isn't just about checking boxes. It's about keeping your people cared for, your message clear, and your staff from stress-eating the leftover communion wafers. Here's how AI can help you simplify the madness:

- **Planning Timelines:** Ask AI to generate a step-by-step timeline for your next event based on the type, size, and date. Want a 10-week planning schedule for VBS with weekly tasks for registration, promotion, volunteer training, and prep? Done in seconds.

- **Event Schedules:** Ask AI to build out a detailed hour-by-hour event schedule based on your vision and goals. Want an outreach night that's high-energy but family-friendly? Or a leadership retreat with breaks, discussion times, and moments of worship? Feed AI your goals and constraints – it'll help structure the flow for maximum impact.

- **Task Lists and Checklists:** AI can help you build scalable prep lists for food, décor, supplies, and more – whether you're planning a marriage conference for 40 or a community cookout for 400.

- **RSVP and Reminder Messaging:** Need to send event invites, confirmations, or reminders that sound warm, fun, and like they came from a human? AI can write those in your tone, whether it's laid-back, heartfelt, or full of emojis.

- **Group Assignments and Rotations:** For Kids and Student Ministry events, use AI to help build groups that balance leader and peer requests, grade levels, allergies, and special needs. What used to take hours of sorting now takes minutes – and the results are more thoughtful, too.

- **Schedule Creation for Staff and Volunteers:** Event staffing can feel like an air traffic control tower. Ask AI to generate personalized schedules that show each volunteer exactly where they need to be and when based on their role. Setup, tear-down, rotation shifts, or teaching times – AI keeps it clear and consistent.

- **Venue Layout & Mapping Suggestions:** Upload your building map, blueprints, or even photos of your lobby, parking lot, or auditorium. Multimodal AI tools (like ChatGPT with image input) can analyze your space and recommend where to place check-in tables, signage, activity zones, or food stations to maximize efficiency and minimize chaos. Who knows - maybe the setup you've used for years isn't the most efficient layout after all. (Don't worry, I'm preaching to myself here too.)

- **Signage and Wayfinding Copy:** Need catchy, clear signage for parking, check-in, or breakout rooms? Ask AI for a signage list and wording suggestions based on your theme or tone. It'll even write the directional arrows for you.

Bonus Tip: Use AI to summarize last year's post-event feedback and generate improvement suggestions. Paste in your volunteer debriefs, survey results, and attendance notes – and ask AI for a list of things to repeat, refine, or rethink.

Event planning will always take effort. But it doesn't have to take your sanity. When you let AI carry the clipboard, you get to lead with creativity, care, and clarity.

Don't Overthink It - Just Start Somewhere

By now, you've seen how AI can support the behind-the-scenes systems that keep ministry running: organizing volunteers, crafting outreach, analyzing growth, building content, and coordinating events. It's a lot to take in – and that's okay.

You don't have to master every area. Just pick the one that feels most overwhelming right now and start there.

It's about finding one place where you feel stuck or tired, and letting AI help you breathe a little easier.

Maybe it's building a better VBS schedule. Or writing your first batch of AI-powered social posts. Or finally getting that guest connection system out of your head and into a workflow.

Start with one step. Test it. See how it helps. Because the purpose of this chapter isn't to wow you with tools – it's to remind you that you don't have to carry everything alone. AI can help you breathe. Focus. Lead more clearly.

And while these tools can optimize your systems, they will never replace what makes ministry powerful: your presence, your discernment, your dependence on the Spirit of God.

So don't wait for perfection. Don't fear the learning curve. Don't get paralyzed by all the possibilities. Just start.

And when you're ready to take it a step further – not just with your operations, but with your people – go ahead and read on. Because the next chapter will show you how AI can support what really matters: your communication, care, discipleship, and leadership development.

CHAPTER 6:
AI IN ACTION, PART TWO – EMPOWERING PEOPLE AND SPIRITUAL GROWTH

Team Communication | Guest Experience | Care & Follow-Up |
Discipleship & Formation | Leadership Development

People Over Process: Tools to Help You Shepherd Well

If Chapter 5 was all about streamlining your systems, Chapter 6 is about strengthening your relationships. You didn't get into ministry for spreadsheets. You're here because people matter. And the pastoral weight of walking with others – through celebration, confusion, burnout, or breakthrough – can't be outsourced.

But what if you had support that allowed you to lead people with more clarity, compassion, and care?

This chapter isn't about removing your humanity –
it's about amplifying it.

With the right tools, you can communicate with more precision, care with more consistency, and disciple with more intentionality. Here's what we'll explore:

1. **Team Communication** – Internal updates, email tone drafting, meeting recaps.

2. **Guest Experience** – Automated workflows for first-time visitors and hospitality improvements.
3. **Care & Follow-Up** – Crafting thoughtful messages for pastoral support, prayer requests, and crisis response.
4. **Discipleship & Formation** – Creating reflection questions, spiritual growth tools, and study resources.
5. **Leadership Development** – Coaching scenarios, performance reviews, and training plans.

This chapter is designed to be practical – but it's also pastoral. Because tools aren't just for getting stuff done. They're for loving people well. You don't need to use everything here. Just start where your heart feels the pull. Let's explore how AI can help you lead people with more wisdom, presence, and peace – one prompt at a time.

1. Team Communication:
From Wordsmithing Stress to Clarity and Care

Internal communication might not be flashy – but it's where ministry lives or dies. Emails, Slack messages, meeting agendas, and team updates are how vision gets shared, decisions get clarified, and expectations get aligned. And too often, they're typed in a hurry, late at night, or in response to someone else's strong emotions.

Here's where AI can help – not to make you sound robotic or inauthentic, but to help you stay clear, kind, and consistent when the stakes are high and your emotions are (understandably) real. Here's how:

- **Clarifying Internal Updates:** Draft Monday morning recaps, pre-service team huddle reminders, or staff-wide memos in a way that's concise but encouraging. Need to clarify something without creating panic? Let AI help you say it in a way that informs and inspires.
- **Tone Check for Difficult Emails:** Ever gotten that email – the critique, the complaint, the one that makes your blood pressure spike? Use AI as a safe place to talk it out. Give a voice memo or a few paragraphs explaining the situation

and your desired tone: "I want to sound pastoral, not defensive." Or "I need to be firm without being harsh." AI can help you workshop a draft or improve your wording to de-escalate and honor the relationship.

- **Writing with Empathy and Clarity:** You don't want to sound cold or overly polished. Tell AI how you want to come across – gracious, confident, kind, apologetic without over-apologizing – and it can help you find words that reflect your heart, not just your stress level.
- **Summarizing Meetings and Notes:** If you've recorded a meeting or taken rough notes, ask AI to clean them up into a clear summary with bullet points, follow-ups, and tone that matches your culture. It can save hours and ensure nothing gets lost between "We should do this" and "Did anyone actually write that down?"

Bonus Tip: If you're unsure how a message will come across, paste your draft into ChatGPT and ask, "How might this be perceived by a parent, volunteer, or team member?" It's like having a built-in communications coach to help you catch blind spots and build trust – before you hit "send".

2. Guest Experience: From First Visit to First Step

We talk a lot about first impressions in ministry – and for good reason. The average guest decides whether they'll come back within *seven minutes*. That's before the message. Before the worship. Sometimes before the coffee even hits the cup.

And let's be honest: we're often so focused on pulling off Sunday that we don't have time to think strategically about what guests experience beyond "smile and wave at the door." That's where AI becomes more than just a clever tool – it becomes a practical partner in crafting a guest experience that's personal, prompt, and intentional. Here's how:

- **Visitor Follow-Up That Feels Like You:** Already mentioned in earlier sections, but worth exploring deeper – AI can help you write warm, personal follow-ups that reflect the tone and heart of your church. Paste in their connection card info, and prompt AI to write a short note: "Write a follow-up email from a Kids Pastor to a first-time family who brought their toddler to church this Sunday. Be warm, specific, and not overly formal."

- **Customized Onboarding Journeys:** Rather than sending every guest the same "Thanks for visiting" message, use AI to craft variations based on their demographics or interests. New to the area? Family with teens? Recent college grad? AI can help generate segmented messaging based on their connection card responses, so people don't just hear from the church – they feel seen by it.

- **Automated First-Timer Workflows:** Let AI help draft a four-touch follow-up sequence after someone's first visit. Think: a text from a volunteer that afternoon, a Monday email with a video from the pastor, a Thursday invite to a Next Steps event, and a follow-up check-in a month later. You can even have AI adjust the tone per platform – friendly text, informative email, heartfelt letter.

- **Hospitality Training Aids:** Want to improve your greeting team's confidence and consistency? Feed your best practices or team guidelines into AI and ask it to create a hospitality cheat sheet or role-play scenarios. You can even say, "Create 5 awkward guest situations and how a greeter should respond with warmth and clarity."

- **Facility and Wayfinding Audits:** Ask AI to help evaluate your physical and digital spaces from a guest's point of view. "What would a first-time parent think walking into this lobby?" or "Critique this welcome page on our website." It can help you spot what's missing, unclear, or intimidating.

- **Guest Experience Surveys:** Want better feedback? Ask AI to generate a 5-question follow-up survey that won't scare guests away. It can even help you analyze those responses for patterns and insights.

- **Language and Accessibility Improvements:** AI can help ensure your communication is clear, welcoming, and inclusive. You can paste your connection card or web welcome text and ask, "How can I make this more accessible to ESL speakers or neurodiverse guests?"

Bonus Tip: Let AI help you map a guest journey from their first Google search to their second visit. You can say, "Create a 10-step guest experience plan for a mid-sized church that includes digital, physical, and relational moments." Use it as a baseline to spark strategy conversations with your team.

3. Care & Follow-Up:
From "Thinking of You" to Thoughtfully With You

At the heart of ministry is *care*. And when someone in your church is navigating crisis, loss, or even a prayer request they trusted you with – your words matter more than ever. But here's the tension: ministry rarely slows down just because someone needs you to say the right thing.

We've all been there. You're racing to your next meeting and staring at a blank screen, trying to respond to a sensitive email from a grieving family or a hurting volunteer. You want to be fully present. You want to be pastoral. But your mental bandwidth is running on fumes. This is where AI can help – not to replace your care, but to help express it clearly, calmly, and compassionately. Here's how AI can support care and follow-up communication:

- **Prayer Request Responses:** Ask AI to help you craft a kind, personalized reply to a submitted prayer request. You can paste the request into ChatGPT and prompt it with: "Write a warm, pastoral response acknowledging their need and expressing support." Then edit it with your personal voice before sending.

- **Crisis Communication Support:** Need to respond to someone navigating job loss, divorce, illness, or family tragedy? Ask AI to generate three tone options for a response – formal, pastoral, and conversational. It'll give you a head start when your emotions are still catching up with your empathy.
- **Tone-Check for Hard Emails:** Whether it's a note to a burned-out volunteer or a reply to a parent who's upset, AI can help you double-check tone. Just ask, "How does this sound? Do I come off defensive?" You'll often catch something you didn't realize was there.
- **Encouragement Templates:** Want to send a short word of encouragement to someone going through a rough time? Ask AI for 5 variations of one-sentence texts that sound personal and sincere, not robotic or canned. Example: "Just wanted you to know I'm praying for you today – your faith in the middle of this season is inspiring."
- **Care Ministry Coordination:** AI can help you organize and document care interactions across a team. Use it to summarize pastoral notes, suggest follow-up timelines, and draft check-in emails or texts that sound human – not like a support ticket auto-response.
- **Volunteer and Team Support:** Pastoral care includes your own team. Use AI to help write thank-you notes, check-ins, or even specific affirmations based on recent conversations. Try prompting: "Help me write a thank-you note for a volunteer who stayed late to clean up after baptism Sunday and is walking through a tough season at home."

Bonus Tip: Use voice input when you're emotionally tired or mentally foggy. Just talk to ChatGPT like you're processing with a trusted friend: "Hey, I need to send a note to Sarah who just lost her dad. I don't want to sound cliché or overly formal. Can you help me write something short and heartfelt?" Then revise until it feels like something you'd truly say.

This is the sacred side of ministry most people don't see – so why not let AI quietly carry a bit of the emotional labor behind the scenes? It's not about making care mechanical. It's about removing barriers to connection so your empathy can lead the way.

4. Discipleship & Formation:
From Generic Resources to Personalized Growth

Discipleship is at the core of the Church's mission – but, in reality, it's easy for this area to feel under-resourced, underdeveloped, and overgeneralized. You want to walk people toward maturity in Christ, but between Sunday's message and next Tuesday's meeting, creating customized tools for spiritual growth can feel like a luxury you don't have time for.

AI can change that. With a few prompts and your ministry vision in mind, you can build thoughtful, personalized discipleship resources that help people reflect, apply, and grow – all without starting from a blank page. Here's how AI can serve your discipleship strategy:

- **Create Reflection Questions:** After you write your sermon or small group lesson, ask AI to generate 5–10 reflection questions based on the core message. Want to focus on application? Ask for "questions that help young adults apply this message to workplace culture." Want to foster deeper group discussion? Ask for "questions that spark vulnerability and honest reflection."

- **Build Reading Plans and Devotionals:** Give AI your teaching theme, and it can generate a 5-day Bible reading plan or a week of short devotionals tied to your series. You can customize tone, format, and audience – whether it's for parents, teens, new believers, or leadership teams.

- **Design Formation Tools for Different Audiences:** Ask AI to rewrite your content for a specific demographic or spiritual maturity level. Need a version of your study guide for middle schoolers? For ESL learners? For new believers just starting their faith journey? You can adapt with ease.
- **Generate Spiritual Habit Trackers and Prompts:** Want to help your congregation develop rhythms of prayer, journaling, or Scripture memory? AI can create printable or digital habit trackers, reminder text templates, or journal prompts based on your discipleship goals.
- **Summarize Theology for Accessibility:** Paste a dense theological paragraph into ChatGPT and ask it to rewrite it at a 6th-grade reading level. Or explain the concept of grace using examples from sports, school, or family life. This is especially useful when helping leaders teach kids, students, or those newer to church culture.
- **Create Companion Tools for Sermon Series:** Ask AI to build small group questions, memory verse cards, family devotionals, or follow-up discussion guides for each week of your message series – customized to the tone and voice of your church.

Bonus Tip: Ask AI to create a discipleship inventory assessment. Give it a few categories you value (e.g., prayer, Scripture, generosity, mission, relationships) and ask it to generate a simple self-evaluation tool with reflection prompts and next steps. You can even ask for a digital version for use in your church app or website.

Discipleship isn't just about information – it's about transformation. And AI won't do the forming for you, but it can help create the scaffolding people need to grow. It can help leaders build environments where reflection becomes a rhythm, and spiritual maturity becomes more accessible than ever.

5. Leadership Development:
From Guesswork to Growth Plans

Raising up leaders is one of the most rewarding – and most time-consuming – parts of ministry. Whether you're coaching a new small group leader, walking alongside a future kids ministry director, or trying to build a pipeline for volunteers to step into greater responsibility, leadership development is often reactive instead of strategic.

AI can help you shift from last-minute improvisation to intentional, thoughtful investment. Here's how AI can support your leadership pipeline:

- **Simulate Coaching Scenarios:** Want to help a new leader think through conflict resolution? Accountability? Vision casting? Ask AI to generate sample leadership scenarios and reflection questions that spark healthy dialogue and growth. You can customize by ministry area, experience level, or topic.

- **Draft Personalized Development Plans:** Based on a leader's strengths, growth areas, and role, AI can help you create a 3-month development roadmap. Include books to read, questions to reflect on, meetings to attend, and skills to practice. You can even generate versions based on different leadership styles or personality types.

- **Create Feedback Templates and Performance Reviews:** Instead of starting from scratch, ask AI to help you build review templates that are kind, honest, and action-oriented. Want a review form that balances encouragement and challenge? Done. Want help phrasing constructive feedback in a way that's specific and grace-filled? Just ask.

- **Design Mini-Trainings for Volunteers:** AI can help you generate bite-sized training modules for first-time team members or new leaders. Ask it to summarize core values, expectations, or even "what to do when" scenarios based on your handbook or culture.

- Curate Resource Lists: Based on a leadership topic (e.g., delegation, time management, or servant leadership), ask AI to recommend podcasts, articles, book excerpts, or case studies to share with your team. You can even have it generate reflection questions or a reading guide.

Bonus Tip: Ask AI to role play a difficult conversation. Want to practice confronting a team member who's consistently late? Or talking to a leader about stepping down for a season? AI can simulate the conversation and offer tips on tone, phrasing, and emotional intelligence. It's not perfect – but it'll help you walk in more prepared and less anxious.

Developing leaders doesn't happen by accident. It takes time, clarity, and consistency. But with the help of AI, you can build a scalable system that doesn't compromise the personal. Instead of relying on charisma or chance, you're cultivating the next wave of leaders with intention - and freeing yourself to focus on the relational investment only you can make.

Let the Tools Serve the Mission – Not the Other Way Around

In this chapter, we moved from systems to shepherding. From emails and workflows to conversations, prayer, and leadership formation. This is where the real heart of ministry beats -and where the right tools, used wisely, can lift your hands without replacing your voice.

If Chapter 5 helped you get organized, Chapter 6 was about helping you stay present. You've seen how AI can help:

- draft sensitive follow-ups with care and clarity,
- personalize your guest journey,
- create discipleship tools that meet people where they are,
- and coach emerging leaders with thoughtfulness and direction.

And if all of that feels like a lot, that's okay. This isn't about doing everything. It's about doing something with intention. Because sometimes the most spiritual thing you can do... is hit "send" on an encouraging message you've been putting off.

Reflection: The Small Wins Still Matter

AI won't make your church healthy.
But it might give you margin to lead toward health.

AI won't do the ministry for you. But it can help you lead it with more presence, more wisdom, and more space for what only you can do. So try the new tool. Prompt the next message. Build the resource that's been sitting in your backlog for months.

Let AI serve your mission – not define it. Because with God's Spirit in you, and the right tools beside you, the small wins will start to stack up. And that's how churches flourish.

CHAPTER 7:
THE POWER OF PROMPT ENGINEERING

Crafting Effective Prompts for Ministry Tools

Unlocking AI's Full Potential – One Prompt at a Time

Let's play a quick game. Have you ever typed something into ChatGPT, hit "send"… and then felt like the response was just meh? You're not alone. The most common phrase I hear from pastors who are trying out AI tools for the first time is: "It was okay, but honestly…I could've just written that myself."

Here's the secret: The difference between "meh" and "mind-blowing" isn't the model. It's the prompt.

It's not that AI doesn't work. It's that we often don't ask in a way that works. Let's continue an analogy that we've already covered: AI is like a seminary intern. Fast. Enthusiastic. Full of potential. And sometimes? *Completely missing the point.*

It's not because they're incapable. It's because you handed them a giant, vague assignment with no structure, no examples, and no direction.

"Hey, go make this great by Tuesday."

"What is 'this'? What is 'great'? And for who?"

But when you give that intern a clear task, a format to follow, a tone to match, and some helpful context? That's when the magic happens. It's the same with ChatGPT.

And here's the funny part: We all know what it's like to have the right tool… and use it completely the wrong way. A few years ago, I needed to remove an old microwave that was built into our kitchen cabinets. No clue how to detach it. No idea where the screws were. No fancy toolkit. But I did have one thing… an axe.

(I'll let that sit for a second.)

So, yes – I "removed" the microwave. Did I technically get the job done? Sure. Did my kitchen cabinets suffer irreparable trauma? Also, yes. The tool wasn't the issue. It was how I used it. That's what this chapter is about. We're not going to get nerdy with syntax. We're not going to turn you into a coder. You don't need to memorize programming language or write semicolons in your sleep.

But you do need to learn how to ask better questions.

Because when it comes to AI, your prompt determines your result.

Think about it this way: The best leaders – the ones who mentor well, inspire teams, and cast compelling vision – aren't always the ones with the most answers. *They're the ones who ask the best questions.*

Prompt engineering is just that: learning to ask great questions. Not because ChatGPT is moody and unpredictable…but because the quality of your input determines the quality of its output. This chapter will help you master that skill. And here's the beautiful part: great prompts aren't just for tech people. They're for everyone:

- The Kids Pastor writing next month's parent email.
- The Admin Assistant creating slides for a last-minute funeral.
- The Worship Leader planning a setlist and needing a fresh Scripture or prayer.

- The Campus Pastor brainstorming how to connect with skeptical guests.

This isn't about being trendy. It's about being intentional. Because AI is here to stay. It'll be built into your software, your workflows, your planning tools, your sermon platforms, and more. And the thing that will set great ministry leaders apart isn't what tools they use - it's *how well they use them*.

AI might not replace your job. But someone who knows how to use it well? They might be the one everyone looks to when it's time to innovate. So, whether you've dabbled in prompts before or you're just opening ChatGPT for the first time, this chapter will give you the confidence, clarity, and creativity to use it well. Let's learn how to unlock AI's full potential – one prompt at a time.

The Four Elements of a Great Prompt

José Antonio Bowen and C. Edward Watson, authors of *Teaching with AI*, outline a fantastic four-part framework designed for educators using AI in the classroom. But I think their structure is spot-on for ministry use, too. Whether you're planning a sermon series or drafting an email to volunteers, the same four elements – **Task, Format, Voice, and Context** – help you get the kind of results that actually sound like you and serve the Church well.

These four steps have helped dozens of ministry leaders immediately improve how they use AI. Let's walk through each one with examples tailored to the church world.

1. Task

What exactly do you want AI to do?

This is where it all begins. Too many prompts sound like, "Help me with this thing." Be specific. Use verbs that point to an action and a result.

Use verbs like: Create, summarize, analyze, elaborate, rewrite, compare, brainstorm, translate, improve, role-play, design, outline

Example:

- Poor: "Write about serving in Kids Ministry."
- Better: "Create a 3-sentence pitch that invites new volunteers to serve in Kids Ministry, emphasizing joy, impact, and team culture."

Pro Tip: The stronger the verb, the more precise the response. Words like "draft," "summarize," "rewrite," "brainstorm," or "compare" give AI a clearer directive than vague phrases like "help me with" or "tell me about."

2. Format
What kind of output are you expecting?

AI doesn't know what shape you want your answer in unless you tell it. Think beyond paragraphs. Consider the structure that will serve your ministry best.

Formats might include: Bullet list, lesson plan, email draft, devotional, script, outline, checklist, slide deck, dialogue, quiz, infographic copy, table, Excel formula, chart

Example:

- Poor: "Can you help me summarize this training manual?"
- Better: "Summarize this 3-page training manual into a volunteer-facing checklist I can print and tape to the prep room wall."

Pro Tip: Add specific quantity indicators - like "5 options," "3 bullets," or "a 2-minute read." It sets guardrails for the AI and keeps things usable in your real-world ministry context.

3. Voice
What style of language or tone do you want it to use?

Tone matters, especially in ministry. Do you want it warm and pastoral? Playful and fun? Serious and reverent? The more detail you provide, the more "you" it will sound. You can prompt with:

- "In the voice of a Kids Pastor"
- "Casual, funny, and upbeat like a Chick-fil-A training video"
- "Warm and pastoral with a touch of humor"
- "Simple enough for a parent reading on their phone during a soccer game"

Example:
- Poor: "Write a message inviting people to serve."
- Better: "Write a message inviting people to serve in Kids Ministry and make it sound like a friendly Kids Pastor who's genuinely excited, slightly goofy, and speaking to a parent who's never volunteered before."

Pro Tip: Upload your past work and ask ChatGPT to match your tone for consistency across platforms. It's a simple way to keep your voice consistent across social media, emails, and even curriculum materials.

4. Context
What background info or examples will help AI respond accurately?

This is the game-changer. Context is what separates "technically correct" responses from "this actually nailed it." It's not just about what you want – it's about the environment you're in, the audience you're serving, and the constraints you're working with. Think of context like setting the stage. If AI is your intern, context is telling them who the message is for, what tone to use, where it's going, what landmines to avoid, and what success looks like.

Some Kids Pastors say, "I don't have time to type all that in!" That's fair. But here's a pro move: just talk to it. Use the ChatGPT voice input feature (that little microphone icon) and explain your scenario like you're leaving a voice memo for a friend. Say what's going on, what you're hoping for, and what you definitely don't want. AI will listen, understand, and give you a better response – faster. Especially if you're an external processor, this can be total magic. Context can be:

- Audience info ("This is for skeptical parents.")
- Constraints ("Only have 150 words.")
- Preferred outcomes ("Must work for ESL readers.")
- Values/mission statements ("Our church tagline is 'Every kid known and loved.'")

Example:
- Poor: "Write a short announcement for church."
- Better: "Write a 2-paragraph announcement for the parent newsletter, inviting families to our new midweek Kids Night. The tone should be friendly and enthusiastic but not pushy. Include the start date, location, and childcare details. This is for busy parents who are overwhelmed with too many emails already – so be clear and brief."

Pro Tip: More context = better answers. You don't need paragraphs – just helpful details.

Sample Prompt Makeover: Before & After

Here's how applying these four elements can transform your results.

- Before: "Help me with a volunteer appreciation idea."
- After: "Brainstorm 5 creative volunteer appreciation ideas for Kids Ministry. Use a warm, budget-friendly tone. Our church is in the Midwest and most of our volunteers are parents. The budget is $50 and we're celebrating during Volunteer Sunday next month. Format the ideas as a bullet list with short explanations."

Night and day.

Real Ministry Prompts – And Why They Matter

Sometimes all it takes is a well-phrased prompt to unlock a solution you didn't think you had time for. Here are a few real-life examples you can try (or adapt) for your own setting:

Example Prompt	"Why It Works"
"Reword this email to sound more gracious and less defensive while still addressing the concern."	Perfect for responding to a frustrated parent, confused team member, or critical church attendee when emotions are running high.
"Create a 60-second script for a video that invites new families to our Easter services. Make it heartfelt, fun, and family-focused."	Quickly drafts content that sounds human, not corporate - and captures your church's voice when your creativity tank is empty.
"Generate 3 sample parent guides based on this Sunday's lesson: Jonah and the Whale (Jonah 1–4). Make one for toddlers, one for kids, and one for preteens."	Shows how one prompt can produce differentiated resources for multiple age groups in just a few seconds.
"Role-play a tough conversation with a Kids Ministry volunteer who's been consistently late. I want to practice how I come across."	You can even simulate tricky leadership conversations – getting feedback on tone, phrasing, and potential responses before the real moment arrives.

Common Prompt Pitfalls

Too vague: "Help me write something for this Sunday."

Instead: "Create a 3-paragraph email that invites our church families to the Fall Fest this Sunday. Include event highlights, parking info, and a warm tone."

Too robotic: "Use professional tone for training."

Instead: "Write a training script for new volunteers in Kids Ministry. Make it friendly, clear, and a little playful so it doesn't feel boring."

Why This Matters More Than Ever

Prompting well is the new literacy. Just like you learned how to write a sermon outline, lead a team meeting, or craft a baptism email – you can learn this too.

Here's the thing: prompt engineering isn't just about better outputs. It's about stewardship. You're not asking AI to be your replacement. You're inviting it into your process as a helper – one that speeds up the admin, sparks creativity, and helps you better love and serve people.

Great prompts let you do more ministry by spending less time stuck. They help you teach clearer, write faster, plan smarter, and communicate more intentionally. And as AI tools continue to develop, your ability to ask the right question may be one of your most valuable leadership skills.

In fact, prompting is quickly becoming the new literacy of the digital age. It's no longer about who has access to the tools. It's about who knows how to use them well. Think of it like the difference between owning a hammer and knowing how to build a house. Plenty of people can open ChatGPT. But leaders who learn to ask with clarity, creativity, and conviction? They're building something that lasts.

A Quick Analogy: The Power Tool and the Purpose

Imagine handing a power drill to a rookie carpenter. If they don't know what they're building, or what bit to use, or how not to strip a screw – it won't matter how powerful the tool is. They'll get frustrated, make a mess, or abandon the project altogether. But in the hands of someone with vision, intent, and practice? That same tool builds a home. AI is your power tool. Prompting is your skillset. Ministry is the home you're building.

Biblical Lens: Wisdom Precedes Words

Proverbs 25:11 says, "A word fitly spoken is like apples of gold in settings of silver." What if that applied to your AI prompts, too? When you ask with discernment – when your words are "fitly spoken" in the form of a clear prompt – you're more likely to receive a response that builds, blesses, and serves with beauty and purpose.

Final Reflection: Prompt with Prayer and Purpose

So before you open ChatGPT next time, take 15 seconds to pause. Ask:

- What do I really want this to do?
- Who is this for?
- What do they need?
- And how can this tool help me serve them better?

Because the best prompt isn't just well-worded. It's Kingdom-minded. Start prompting like a pastor, not a programmer.

CHAPTER 8:
AI'S LIMITATIONS AND HUMAN UNIQUENESS

Why Technology Can Never Replace Pastoral Care

The Imago Dei in a Digital Age

Let's get this out of the way: I love AI. I genuinely believe it can radically simplify systems, unlock creative energy, and serve the Church in deeply meaningful ways. I've used it to streamline volunteer communication, rewrite lesson plans, brainstorm big events, and even reflect on hard conversations. It's a tool I return to again and again.

But no matter how smart the tools get, no matter how fast they work or how convincingly human they sound, AI will never be made in the image of God. *We are.* And that truth sits at the heart of this chapter.

Because for all the breakthroughs AI brings to ministry, it also brings a clear boundary line. A necessary one. There is a difference between help and replacement. Between support and surrender. AI can help you plan an event. It cannot pray with the grieving. It can organize data and surface insights. It cannot see the pain behind someone's eyes. That distinction isn't a technical issue. It's a theological one.

This is not merely about the limitations of AI. It's about the design of creation. God didn't outsource His love for people to a digital assistant. He entrusted it to you. AI does not carry the Imago Dei. But you do. Your volunteers do. Every kid in your ministry, every parent in your church, every staff member and skeptical guest walking through your doors bears the image of God.

> That means the most powerful force in ministry is still presence.
> Not processing power.

As I said in the introduction, and it bears repeating here: *No machine can replace the spiritual discernment, emotional intelligence, pastoral care, and relational presence of a human being.*

Let me put it another way: How would you feel if a deeply personal interaction turned out to be robot-driven? Imagine this. You're going through a hard season. A friend sends you a long, heartfelt message that brings you to tears. It feels like exactly what you needed. Maybe it helped you breathe again. Maybe it gave you the strength to keep going. You reply to say thank you, and they casually respond, "Oh yeah, I asked ChatGPT to write that for you."

Suddenly the words that felt sacred begin to feel synthetic. You might smile and brush it off, but deep down? You'd feel a pang of betrayal. A letdown. A strange mix of embarrassment, confusion, and loss. Because something you thought was deeply personal turned out to be copy-paste.

We all crave authenticity. When that trust is broken, especially in emotionally significant moments, it's not just a misstep. It feels like a violation of something sacred.

So let's be clear. I'm not calling for a rejection of AI. I'm calling for a right placement of it. Let it support your ministry, not impersonate it. Let it amplify your ideas, not substitute your presence. Let it hold the clipboard, not the microphone. In the rest of this chapter, we'll unpack where the line is, and how to make sure we stay on the side of faithfulness, not just functionality.

Because the Church doesn't need more *content*. It needs more *connection*. And no machine, no matter how advanced, can embody what Christ has placed within you.

Why Lived Presence Still Matters

You've heard the message throughout this chapter: AI can assist with tasks, but it cannot replace your presence. It can draft a follow-up email or help you outline a message, but it cannot grieve, hug, listen, or weep. Because there is a chasm between knowing something and experiencing it.

There's a scene in the movie Good Will Hunting that captures this truth perfectly. Robin Williams plays a therapist named Sean who meets Will, a brilliant but guarded 20-year-old janitor at MIT played by Matt Damon. Will is a genius. He has an incredible memory, a photographic mind, and has read more books than most professors. But he is also wounded, defensive, and emotionally shut down.

During their first meetings, Will deflects, postures, and hides behind his intelligence. He throws out quotes, facts, and theories to avoid vulnerability. But Sean doesn't buy it. In one pivotal moment, they sit together on a bench in Boston's Public Garden. What follows is a monologue that cuts through Will's intellect and confronts his lack of lived experience.

Here's part of the famous monologue:

Robin Williams (Sean): *So if I asked you about art, you'd probably give me the skinny on every art book ever written. Michelangelo, you know a lot about him. Life's work, political aspirations, him and the pope, sexual orientations, the whole works, right? But I'll bet you can't tell me what it smells like in the Sistine Chapel. You've never actually stood there and looked up at that beautiful ceiling, seen that.*

If I ask you about women, you'd probably give me a syllabus of your personal favorites. You may have even been laid a few times. But you can't tell me what it feels like to wake up next to a woman and feel truly happy.

You're a tough kid. And I'd ask you about war, you'd probably throw Shakespeare at me, right? "Once more unto the breach, dear friends." But you've never been near one. You've never held your best friend's head in your lap and watched him gasp his last breath, looking to you for help.

I'd ask you about love, you'd probably quote me a sonnet. But you've never looked at a woman and been totally vulnerable. Known someone that could level you with her eyes. Feeling like God put an angel on Earth just for you. Who could rescue you from the depths of hell. And you wouldn't know what it's like to be her angel. To have that love for her be there forever. Through anything. Through cancer.

And you wouldn't know about sleeping sitting up in a hospital room for two months holding her hand because the doctors could see in your eyes that the terms "visiting hours" don't apply to you. You don't know about real loss. Because that only occurs when you love something more than you love yourself. I doubt you've ever dared to love anybody that much.

This moment in the film is unforgettable because it strips away the illusion that knowledge and data can replace lived experience and real presence. Will may have all the intelligence in the world, but he hasn't yet learned what it means to be with someone in their suffering.

Sound familiar? This is exactly what makes pastoral care irreplaceable. No algorithm can offer this kind of raw, Spirit-empowered, eye-to-eye ministry. No chatbot can replicate that kind of love. This is the work that AI can't do. This is what it means to bear the image of God in the face of another.

A Story from the Frontlines

A few years ago, there was a school shooting at the middle school closest to my house. It wasn't just close in proximity, it was personal. All of the neighborhood kids we'd come to know and love were inside that building when it happened. Kids who played basketball in our driveway. Kids who made chalk art on our street. Kids who walked past our house every weekday morning with backpacks too big for their frames and eyes too bright for the tragedy that was about to unfold.

That day was chaos wrapped in silence. I remember walking outside and realizing that our entire neighborhood had done the same. No one planned it. No one sent a text or rang a doorbell. But we all ended up on our driveways, shoulder to shoulder but emotionally unraveling.

Some stood with arms crossed, trying to keep it together. Others sat on the curb, heads in their hands, visibly shaking. Many of us were holding each other, praying without words. A few were whispering updates. Most of us were just looking down the street toward the school we could no longer see the same way again.

We were crying. We were angry. We were confused. We didn't have answers. We didn't need to. We just needed to be there.

That evening, we opened our church. Not for a production. Not for a plan. Just for people. We turned the lights low, set out tissue boxes, lit a few candles, and opened the doors. No one was checking head counts. No one was taking notes. There wasn't a script or a sermon. Just space. Just silence. Just the shared ache of a community trying to breathe again.

And then came Sunday. I'll never forget it. It wasn't a "normal" service. There was no clever bumper video or smooth transition from worship to message. That morning, the songs were quieter. The room was heavier.

We gathered the kids, just like we always did, but nothing about it was routine. Our team sat with them on the floor. We looked them in the eyes. We told them the truth about God and His character – how He is still good, even when the world is not. How He is near to the brokenhearted. How Jesus Himself cried when His friend died. We reminded them that tears are holy, and that silence isn't empty, it can be sacred.

We didn't read from a pre-written devotional or ask them to fill out reflection cards. We didn't hand out coloring pages about peace or package this pain into neat, teachable moments. We just held each other. Some kids asked hard questions. Some didn't say a word. Some cried in our arms. Others kicked a ball outside, needing to process the only way their little bodies knew how.

And we let them. We let them feel it. We gave them space to mourn, not manage. We offered our presence, not our productivity. Because that's what they needed. And honestly? That's what we needed too.

I don't remember the songs we sang that day. I don't remember what was preached from the stage. But I do remember the weight of the silence, the sound of kids weeping in the arms of volunteers, and the look on a parent's face when someone said, "You don't have to do this alone."

It was one of the most deeply human moments I've ever experienced in ministry. And I can say with complete confidence: no AI model could have guided us through that. No digital devotional could have carried the weight of what those kids and families were feeling. No clever script or chatbot-generated content could have matched the sacredness of standing in the mess and simply being present.

That's ministry. That's the Imago Dei on full display. And that's why this matters so much.

Because when the world breaks,
people don't need a perfect answer.
They need a faithful presence.

When Ministry Isn't a Performance
(Even When You're in Costume)

Let me confess something that might surprise you: I've spent more time than I care to admit dressed as a giant bird.

I was a professional mascot for nearly two decades. I've sweated through fur suits in 90-degree parades, high-fived thousands of kids, and danced badly (but with gusto) at countless events. And during those years, I learned something unexpected: when you're in costume, people assume you're invincible. They project joy, silliness, confidence -all the things they want to see – onto a character. And while that worked great for a halftime show, it didn't help much in ministry.

Because the moment I stepped into Kids Ministry, I realized: real connection doesn't happen when you're playing a part. It happens when you take off the costume.

In pastoral care, there's no script. There are no rehearsed dances or choreographed laughs. There's just you, showing up – sometimes clumsy, sometimes quiet, sometimes unsure – but real. Present. Willing to be fully there.

I say this to remind you (and me): ministry isn't performance. It's presence. You don't need the mascot suit. You don't need to be impressive. You just need to be there and be real.

Theology of Presence

We serve a God who didn't just send a message, He came in person. The Gospel doesn't begin with a broadcast or a post. It begins with presence.

Jesus didn't email the Sermon on the Mount or livestream His parables from a studio. He didn't Zoom into the Last Supper. He came close. He touched the sick, even when others recoiled. He wept with the grieving, even when He knew resurrection was around the corner. He placed His hands on lepers, shared meals with sinners, and knelt beside broken people who had been cast out by society.

> The Savior of the world didn't choose efficiency. He chose embodiment.

Incarnation is at the heart of the Gospel. That's not just theology - it's ministry philosophy. And in an age where digital convenience is king, that incarnational approach is more needed than ever. People want to be seen. Heard. Known. No AI model - no matter how fast, advanced, or impressive - can incarnate that kind of love. It can't show up. It can't sit quietly. It can't bear witness to pain.

No mascot suit could've prepared me for what it's like to walk into a hospital room. Sometimes it was a child clinging to life. Other times it was a parent hearing their final diagnosis. I'd walk in carrying so much pressure. I wanted to say something profound, something theologically sound, something that would somehow hold the weight of the moment. But often, nothing felt like enough.

Then a mentor shared something that forever changed how I see those sacred spaces. He reminded me of the *theology* of presence. He said, "Anthony, when you walk into that room, you're not walking in alone. The Spirit who raised Christ from the dead walks in with you. Your pastoral presence represents the presence of God in the room." Romans 8:11 says, "The Spirit of Him who raised Jesus from the dead is living in you."

And in Matthew 10:19-20, Jesus comforts His disciples with this truth: "Do not worry about what to say or how to say it. At that time you will be given what to say, for it will not be you speaking, but the Spirit of your Father speaking through you." That's the promise. That's the posture.

I began to realize I didn't need to have the perfect words. I just needed to show up. My role was not to impress, explain, or even ease the pain. It was to be present. To bring the Spirit of God into a room aching for peace. Sometimes that meant praying with words. Sometimes it meant sitting in silence. But always, it meant choosing to be fully there.

Ministry is not about perfect phrasing or polished delivery. It's about presence. And if you're called to shepherd people, then your presence – your Spirit-filled, faithful, fully human presence – might be the most powerful tool you carry into any situation.

AI can write scripts. It can draft prayers and organize visitations. But it can't walk into a hospital room and carry hope. That's something only image-bearers can do. That's something only you can do.

A Pastoral Warning

This is a warning we cannot afford to ignore. As AI becomes more capable, the temptation to fake it becomes more subtle and more seductive. You can preload your weekly emails, automate social media for months in advance, generate a year's worth of devotionals, and use AI to mimic warmth and wisdom with a few well-worded prompts. All of this can be done in the name of "efficiency." And yet, you might never once sit across the table from a person far from God and disciple them into a passionate relationship with Jesus.

The danger is not just in the delegation. The danger is in the slow erosion of your authenticity.

When ministry leaders rely more on automation than incarnation, more on programming than presence, we stop pastoring.
We start performing.

We've already seen examples of this in culture. A best man speech delivered by ChatGPT. A eulogy written by an algorithm. It always leaves people unsettled, even hurt. Because something sacred is happening in those moments, and when it's handed off to a machine, it feels hollow. It feels dishonest. No matter how well-written it is, it cannot replicate what the moment demands: a human presence who genuinely cares.

Don't turn into the Wizard of Oz. He had all the bells and whistles, the smoke and the show. But behind the curtain, he was just a frightened man hiding behind a machine. He depended so much on the spectacle that he forgot how to simply be real. Eventually, he built a facade so big that he lost sight of who he was supposed to be.

Let's not make that same mistake in ministry. There is no tool, no matter how polished, that can replace the power of your authentic presence. The Church doesn't need more smoke and mirrors. It needs shepherds. It needs people who will show up, take off the mask, and do the slow, faithful work of walking with others.

And that's good news – it means the work you're doing matters more than ever. Your faithful presence, your quiet consistency, your willingness to sit with people in their pain…it still changes lives.

Hebrews 13:17 reminds us, "They keep watch over you as those who must give an account." As ministry leaders, we will one day stand before God and answer for how we shepherded His people. We won't be held accountable for how many followers we gained, how efficient our systems were, or how polished our content looked. We will be held accountable for the souls we were entrusted with.

So do not lose your soul in the name of scale. Let the tools support your ministry but never let them replace your humanity.

What Only You Can Do

There are some things no AI will ever be able to do. It will never sense the Holy Spirit whispering to you in the middle of a conversation. It will never notice a flicker of fear behind someone's forced smile or feel a gut check when a moment requires silence instead of a solution. It will never feel the lump in your throat when you baptize a child you've prayed for over the years, or the trembling in your hand when you anoint someone who's walking through grief.

AI will never walk a widow out to her car in the rain. It will never pause a sermon to respond to the tears in the room. It will never linger after church just to talk with someone who doesn't know where else to go. It will never offer a shaky, heartfelt apology that comes from conviction, not code.

It will never bend down to pray over a child who is struggling with anxiety, or pace in the hallway while waiting on news from the operating room. It won't show up early to set up chairs just because it honors the team. It won't call a volunteer just to say thank you, with no hidden agenda. It won't listen to someone's story for the sixth time because they needed to say it again. And again. And again.

AI will never hug someone who just gave their life to Jesus. It may generate great content, but it cannot generate compassion. It may write impressive devotionals, but it cannot intercede with tears. It may be able to process tone, but it will never carry presence.

These aren't sentimental extras. This is ministry. This is the real work. AI isn't built for that. Because it's not built for love. It's built for logic. But ministry isn't logical. It's deeply relational. It's messy, intuitive, Spirit-led, and filled with holy interruptions.

Only people – people filled with the Spirit of God – can carry that kind of love into the room. And only you can respond to the nudge that says, "Slow down. Stay here. Be present." Because only you were made in the image of God.

Use It. Don't Depend On It.

Let's be clear: I'm not asking you to toss out the tools. I've said it before and I'll say it again: AI is the ultimate sous-chef. It can chop the vegetables, prep the sauces, set the table, and even offer a creative twist on the menu. It saves time, sharpens your process, and frees you to focus on what only you can do. But here's the thing: **AI doesn't run the kitchen.** You're still the head chef. You make the final call. You taste the dish. You serve the people. The sous-chef supports your creativity – it doesn't replace your leadership.

AI was never meant to carry the weight of your pastoral calling. It's here to hold your clipboard, not your convictions. That means we need to constantly evaluate how we're using it. Not just if we're using AI, but why. What is it replacing? And what is it making possible?

> There's a difference between using a tool to enhance your love for people and using a tool to escape your responsibility to them.

One is stewardship. The other is avoidance.

Here's a helpful gut check you can return to anytime:

- Are you using AI to create clarity in your sermon prep so you can spend more time with people? Or are you automating your way out of personal connection?
- Are you letting it write a recap email so you can call a volunteer and thank them in real time? Or are you using it to stay distant and efficient?
- Are you automating reminders so nothing falls through the cracks? Or are you automating relationships that were never meant to be transactional?

One of the most dangerous things a leader can do is confuse proficiency with presence. Just because something is polished and fast doesn't mean it's faithful. So ask yourself regularly: *Am I handing off something sacred? Or am I freeing myself up to be more present where it counts?*

If the tool helps you love better, use it without apology. But if it's starting to replace the most human parts of your leadership, that's a red flag. Step back. Reevaluate. Refocus. Because tools were always meant to serve the mission, not steer it. And the moment they start doing the leading, we've already missed the point entirely.

A Word About Vulnerability

There's one more thing AI will never be able to do – something that just might be your most powerful pastoral tool: it cannot be vulnerable.

AI can simulate vulnerability. It can mimic the cadence of emotional storytelling. It can write in a tone that sounds raw or honest. But at the end of the day, it doesn't feel anything. It's not carrying grief. It's not wrestling with insecurity. It doesn't know what it means to hope, to doubt, to heal, or to fail. You do. That's not a liability. That's a gift.

Ministry isn't built on polished performance. It's built on courageous presence. When you show up as a leader and choose to be vulnerable (not performative, but honest) people lean in. Not because your life is perfect, but because they can see themselves in your story. Your honesty gives others permission to be honest too.

I've learned this the hard way. In moments when I've tried to impress, I might have earned a few claps. But in moments when I've let down the walls and shared my own questions, struggles, and even failures, that's when real ministry happened. That's when someone would come up after service and say, "Thank you... I thought I was the only one."

Authenticity builds bridges. And in a digital world filled with filters, facades, and algorithmically curated perfection, the Church must be the place where people are reminded what it means to be fully human... and fully loved.

So yes, let AI check your grammar. Let it reword your outline or fix your formatting. But don't let it touch the parts of your story that need to be told with trembling hands and a Spirit-filled heart. Because vulnerability is not a glitch in your leadership. It's your greatest strength.

How to Use AI and Still Stay Human

AI is an incredible tool – but like any tool, *how* you use it matters more than simply *that* you use it. It can either help you become more present in your ministry or slowly pull you away from the very people you're called to love.

The good news? Staying grounded isn't complicated. It just takes intentionality. Here are a few practical reminders for using AI while staying fully human and fully Spirit-led in the process:

Use it for what it's good at.

Let AI carry the weight of systems, structure, and first drafts. It excels at writing meeting agendas, editing announcement slides, brainstorming sermon titles, summarizing notes, and helping you get unstuck creatively. If it saves you an hour you used to spend tweaking your newsletter, and now you spend that hour mentoring a new volunteer or praying with a family – praise God. That's a win. Use the tool where it works best.

Draw the line at pastoral care.

This is the line that matters most. AI can help draft a thoughtful thank-you note or smooth out the tone in a follow-up email. But when you're crafting a funeral sermon or preparing to meet with someone whose marriage is falling apart, AI has no place leading that conversation. Be cautious. Be wise. Don't let the convenience of a helpful draft pull you away from the sacred responsibility of showing up. One-on-one ministry isn't about efficiency. It's about presence.

Pray before you prompt.

This may sound simple, but it's transformational. Before you open a new tab or start typing your request, pause. Take ten seconds. Ask the Holy Spirit to lead you. Invite Him into the creative process. He's not waiting on the sidelines while you innovate. He's in the room with you. You're not just producing content. You're building the Church. So let your prompts begin with prayer. Because it's not all on you - but it's not all on the AI either.

Audit your usage.

Every few months, stop and reflect. This is especially important for ubiquitous, groundbreaking innovations like AI. Pull out a journal or sit with your team and ask honest questions: Am I using this to love people better? Or am I starting to rely on it to avoid difficult conversations? Has it made my messages sharper, or has it started to dull my personal conviction? Are my sermon examples more relevant or just more robotic? No shame here, just awareness. Technology doesn't drift us toward apathy overnight. It happens slowly. But if you catch the drift early, you can course-correct before anything sacred gets lost.

Let AI support your humanity, not replace it.

This is the big idea that undergirds it all. AI should never be the thing that distances you from people. It should be the thing that clears the path for deeper connection. It's not here to replace your mind, your heart, or your Spirit-led discernment. It's just here to hold the clipboard so you can go love the people God has put in your path.

So take the time to reflect. Invite the Spirit to guide. Draw the line when needed. And never forget, your humanity is your superpower.

Final Reflection: The God Who Drew Near

Jesus could have stayed distant. He could have sent prophets, letters, fire from heaven, or visions in the sky. He could have loved us from afar – managed our spiritual development like an overseer checking in occasionally from a remote location. But He didn't. He came close. He chose incarnation.

The Word became flesh and made His dwelling among us – not as a concept, but as a person. Not as a voice in the clouds, but as a man who laughed, touched, healed, wept, and walked among the broken. He sat at tables. He looked people in the eyes. He washed feet. He suffered with and for us. He made His love tangible.

Because when it comes to love, you go yourself.

I remember hearing a pastor once say, "If I need to deliver a message to someone, I'll gladly have someone else pass it along. But if it's an act of love? I'm going myself." That hit me hard. Because it's true.

When I asked my wife to marry me, I didn't send someone else in my place. I didn't outsource the moment. I went myself. I got down on one knee. I looked her in the eye. I offered my words, my thoughts, my heart, my whole self. Because that's what love does.

Love shows up. In person. Without shortcuts. Without efficiency metrics. That's what Jesus did. He didn't send a substitute. He didn't dispatch an ambassador. He came Himself. Fully God, fully man. Not just to say "I love you," but to embody it.

And if we're going to lead like Him, we must resist the temptation to automate everything sacred.

Ministry is not a performance to be perfected,
it is a presence to be lived out.

The Imago Dei reminds us that what matters most in ministry isn't how quickly we can finish a task or how polished our words appear. What matters most is who we are when we show up to love, listen, and serve.

Ministry is about embodiment. It's about being there. It's about real tears in hospital rooms and real joy in baptisms. It's about the quiet comfort of sitting in silence with someone who has no words left. It's about the sacred weight of showing up – again and again – because that's what Jesus did for us.

AI may be able to help you organize, brainstorm, or generate ideas faster than ever before. And yes, it might even help you extend your reach. But it will never replace your reach into the lives of real people. That kind of reach – the ministry of being fully present, fully human, and fully Spirit-led – simply cannot be replicated. It can only be embodied.

So let AI be your tool. Let it hold your notes, draft your outlines, send your reminders. Let it do what it does best: assist, support, and suggest.

As you plan this week's services, pause and ask:
"Where am I tempted to automate
what God has asked me to embody?"

But let your humanity be your ministry. Because that's where the Kingdom breaks through. In the presence of a God who came close. And in His people, who keep showing up.

CHAPTER 9:
LEADING YOUR CHURCH INTO THE AI AGE

How to Introduce Innovation Without Losing Trust

The Hesitancy Is Real

You might be reading this chapter as an early adopter. Maybe you've already tinkered with ChatGPT for your sermon outlines, used AI to summarize parent feedback from your last event, or even recorded a video of yourself speaking Spanish without ever conjugating a single verb. You're not just curious – you're convinced. You see the potential, and you're ready to run.

But here's the thing: most of the people around you probably aren't. Remember earlier in the book when we referenced Barna's 2023 study? According to that research, 3 out of 4 practicing Christians express some level of hesitancy or concern about the rise of artificial intelligence. And among pastors, that number climbs even higher. It's a sobering stat, but also an important one to name as we talk about implementation.

Truth is, by the time you're reading this, those numbers may have shifted. Maybe dramatically. That's the challenge with writing a book about a technology moving faster than a toddler with a box of crayons and a newly painted white wall. Any statistic I cite could already be outdated. So instead of clinging too tightly to the numbers, let's focus on the undercurrent:

---

most people aren't just skeptical of new tools.
They're cautious of what those tools might change.

More Than a Tool: It's a Trust Issue

Adopting new technology is never just about utility. It's about identity. It's about trust. It's about theology. When you bring up AI in your staff meeting, your team probably isn't wondering, "Can this help us?" They're wondering, "Is this still us?"

And those aren't silly questions. They're sacred ones. When AI enters the room, it doesn't just raise questions about productivity. It raises questions about presence, purpose, and what it means to be faithful shepherds of real people. So if you feel resistance, don't be surprised. And don't bulldoze over it either. The Church has a long history of wrestling with change. And the best leaders? They don't run ahead alone. They bring people with them.

So how do you do that? How do you introduce something new without compromising what's sacred? How do you invite your team to try a tool that sounds like science fiction? And how do you avoid the extremes of panic or passivity?

In this chapter, we're going to get real practical. Not on how to prompt or produce, but on how to lead. Because introducing AI into your ministry isn't just a tech move – it's a leadership moment.

To help guide us, I want to borrow a time-tested framework: **John Kotter's 8 Steps for Leading Change**. I've used this model in organizational transitions before, but it's especially helpful now, as we begin to reimagine what faithful innovation can look like in the Church.

So, whether you're leading a Kids Ministry team, a creative arts department, a staff of 25, or just trying to convince one skeptical board member, it's time to put this model to work. Let's walk through it together.

Step 1: Create a Sense of Urgency

Change doesn't start with data. It starts with a story. A reason. A sense that *the cost of staying the same* is greater than *the cost of changing*.

For me, that urgency didn't come from reading a white paper or watching a futuristic documentary. It came from a staff meeting – specifically, from watching a clip of myself preaching on a Sunday and realizing I had said the word "like" no fewer than ninety-four times. I had no idea I was doing it. But with the help of a free AI-powered communication coaching tool, I not only caught the pattern, I learned how to tighten my communication in a way that helped people stay with me longer. That one moment sparked curiosity among our team. Not just because it was humbling (and, like, slightly hilarious), but because it showed them the value right away. This wasn't gimmicky. It was genuinely helpful. And it made people wonder: *Could this help me get better too?*

That's how urgency begins. Not with a guilt trip, but with a glimpse. A glimpse of what's possible. A glimpse of how this tool, when used with wisdom, could actually help us love people better and grow in the work God has called us to do.

You don't need to scare people into change. But you do need to help them see what's at stake. If we're not helping the Church understand this tool, then who will? If we're not leading the charge to steward it wisely, then what narratives will take its place? Urgency isn't about panic. It's about mission. And that's always worth responding to.

Step 2: Build a Guiding Coalition

Change isn't a solo sport. It needs early adopters. Champions. Trusted voices. I started small. With my Kids Ministry team. I showed them what AI could do: help with scheduling headaches, translate parent emails, summarize feedback, and build better follow-up systems. Once they saw the time-saving power, they were in. Not because I made them. But because they felt it.

Then, slowly, other staff members took notice. Someone would say, "Hey, where did you find that VBS theme song so fast?" or "Did you really just make a cowboy jingle about our staff meeting?" They laughed, sure. But it got their attention. And laughter, by the way, is a great way to disarm fear.

One day I showed them a video where I was speaking fluently in Spanish, Japanese, German, and English. "I didn't become a polyglot overnight," I clarified. "That was AI." But I was quick to explain my why: because I want every parent to hear our mission in their heart language. That built trust. Because it wasn't about the tool. It was about the people.

So if you're the only one on your team using AI right now, start inviting others into the conversation. Share small wins. Ask for input. Let them see the potential for themselves. Your job isn't just to lead – it's to multiply momentum.

Step 3: Form a Strategic Vision and Initiatives

Vision matters. People need more than "Hey, I found this cool thing." They need clarity. Direction. A sense of what the future could look like and how AI fits into it.

For me, that vision became simple: Let's steward innovation so we can focus more on what only we can do: being fully present, loving people well, and sharing the Gospel with clarity and creativity. And from that vision came simple initiatives:

- Use AI to summarize parent focus groups instead of spending hours in debrief meetings.

- Use AI to generate draft training outlines, freeing up time for team development.
- Use AI to create kid-friendly content that communicates our values in new ways.

The vision wasn't to become an "AI church." It was to become a more effective, Spirit-led church – one that uses its resources wisely so we can steward people well.

Step 4: Enlist a Volunteer Army

This is where it gets fun. Not everyone needs to be an expert. But everyone can participate. I've started creating low-pressure moments in meetings where we use AI together. I'll say, "Hey, instead of spending the next hour brainstorming from scratch, I asked AI for a list of ideas based on our theme and values. Here's what it came up with. Let's start from here."

People lean in. They're intrigued. Sometimes they're amazed. Sometimes they're skeptical. But either way, they're involved. And that's the win.

We recently ran a SWOT analysis after interviewing parents about our kids ministry experience. Normally, compiling all those transcripts and surfacing patterns would have taken hours of post-meeting synthesis. But this time? I uploaded everything into an AI meeting assistant, and by Monday morning, we had a full breakdown of strengths, weaknesses, opportunities, and threats. It was smart. It was fast. And best of all, our team was shocked…and relieved. We didn't skip the hard conversations. We just skipped the grunt work.

Here's a guiding principle I come back to again and again: AI can get you 60% of the way there. That means the prep work, the drafts, the structure, the raw ideas – AI handles that. Then you, and your human team, do the part only humans can do. You refine. You decide. You collaborate. You discern.

This kind of collaborative starting point lowers the intimidation factor. People don't have to be "tech people." They just have to be curious. When they see AI as a springboard instead of a threat, they realize it's not replacing them. It's equipping them.

So invite others to prompt. To play. To co-create. The more people experience it, the less they fear it and the more momentum you'll build together.

Step 5: Remove Barriers

Fear is one of the biggest barriers to any kind of change. But so is confusion. Unclear expectations, theological questions, technical hurdles – all of these can stop momentum cold. That's why I've tried to be relentlessly transparent.

When I create training materials using AI, I tell my team. When I generate curriculum content or reword a policy, I say, "I used AI for this. Here's why." I don't hide the tool. I explain it. I normalize it.

And most importantly, I constantly clarify what AI can do and what it cannot. I remind our staff and volunteers that I will never use AI to write a eulogy. I will never use it to replace a pastoral visit or a meaningful face-to-face conversation. It's not here to replace our calling. It's here to protect it.

Removing barriers means creating safety. The more your team trusts your motives, the more they'll embrace your methods.

When you remove fear and clarify the why, people stop seeing AI as a threat and start seeing it as a teammate.

Step 6: Generate Short-Term Wins

People need to see results. Not in five years. In five minutes. One of the first "wins" I shared with our staff was a bit silly: a song I generated using AI based entirely on inside jokes from our team meetings. It was fast, funny, and weirdly well-written. Everyone laughed. It was memorable. And more importantly, it showed that this tool wasn't threatening. It was creative. Collaborative. It felt fun again.

But the deeper wins are what built real trust. One of the kids at our church is on the autism spectrum and learns incredibly well through kinesthetic activities. But like most church curricula, ours was largely designed for auditory and discussion-based learners. So instead of rewriting an entire lesson from scratch, I asked AI to help. I uploaded the core teaching points and prompted it to offer alternative ways to present the material using movement, hands-on activities, and visual storytelling.

Within minutes, I had a handful of adaptations that aligned perfectly with what we were already teaching – just designed for a different learning style. We tried one that Sunday. And it worked.

The child who normally disengaged during the Bible story lit up. He was engaged, focused, even excited. His parent pulled me aside after service and said, "I've never seen him this dialed in before. Thank you for seeing him." That was a win.

Not because it was flashy. Not because it saved time. But because it allowed us to love a child in a way that honored his God-given wiring. And all it took was a simple tool, a thoughtful prompt, and a willingness to try.

This is the power of small victories. They don't have to be big to be meaningful. But they do need to be visible. Celebrate them. Tell the stories. Let people see the fruit. Because fruit builds momentum.

Step 7: Sustain Acceleration

The danger with any new tool is novelty fatigue. You start strong. Then the energy dips. People lose interest. They default back to what they know.

So how do you keep momentum going? Two ways: First, keep training. Don't assume your team will just pick this up intuitively. Offer prompts. Host workshops. Share best practices. Give examples. And keep learning together. (You might even start a "Prompt of the Month" to keep it fresh.)

Second, tell stories. Keep sharing real examples of how AI is serving your ministry. That's how culture changes – not by policies, but by repeated storytelling.

Step 8: Anchor the Change in Culture

This is the long game. You know AI is truly integrated when it becomes invisible – not because it's hidden, but because it's part of how you work.

In our Kids Ministry, it's become second nature to use AI for planning, feedback, and follow-up. Not as a gimmick, but as a rhythm. When someone new joins the team, they see right away: this is a place that values innovation, stewardship, and spirit-led creativity.

But we never talk about AI in isolation. We talk about how it helps us do what matters most. And that's the key. Innovation must always point to mission. Culture must always orbit around purpose.

So anchor it in your values. Tie it back to your theology. Remind people, again and again, that this isn't about faster ministry, it's about faithful ministry.

Final Encouragement: You're Not Crazy for Trying

If you're feeling like you're alone in this journey, or like you're dragging your team toward something they don't understand yet…take heart. Leading change is hard. It always has been. Whether you're introducing livestreams, moving check-in to tablets, updating your giving platform, or experimenting with AI – you're going to face resistance. That's not a sign of failure. It's a sign that you're leading.

Just remember: change isn't about convincing everyone overnight. It's about creating space. Casting vision. Building trust. Sharing stories. And showing up with patience, humility, and a clear sense of why this matters.

AI is not the Gospel. But it is a tool that can serve the Gospel. And if we can learn how to lead through it wisely, lovingly, and faithfully, we might just open up doors for more people to hear and experience the hope of Jesus in ways they've never encountered before.

So keep going. Keep learning. Keep inviting others into the journey. Lead with love. Lead with clarity. And lead with the Spirit.

Because the future of the Church isn't just about what tools we use. It's about how we use them to love like Jesus.

CHAPTER 10:
A FAITHFUL FUTURE

How to Innovate with Heart, Hope, and Holy Imagination

The Moment We're In

If you've made it this far, you're not just skimming headlines. You're leaning in. You've stayed with me through prompts and pitfalls, ethical dilemmas and practical wins. You care. Not just about technology, but about people. About the mission. About leading your church, your team, your ministry with wisdom and integrity in an age where the ground beneath our feet feels like it's shifting faster than ever.

This is no small thing. You've navigated pages filled with both encouragement and caution. You've wrestled with possibilities, felt the tension between progress and presence, and asked the hard questions about what it means to be human in a world that increasingly feels automated.

Welcome to the moment we're in. It's not a moment for easy answers or sweeping declarations. It's a moment for leaders like you who are willing to ask, *"What does faithfulness look like now?"*

Because this is a noisy moment. Everyone has an opinion. Open your news feed, and you'll see the same technology described as both the greatest threat to humanity and the most important breakthrough since electricity. AI is going to save us. AI is going to destroy us. Meanwhile, most of us are just trying to figure out how to send an email that doesn't end up in the spam folder.

And in the middle of that noise stands the Church. Our calling hasn't changed, but the tools we use to fulfill that calling have. That's always been true. From scrolls to the printing press. From radio waves to livestreams. From handwritten letters to social media. The Gospel doesn't change, but the methods certainly do. The mission is timeless. The strategies? They adapt.

Here's the tension: the Church is called to be anchored in the eternal and attentive to the cultural. We are stewards of both truth and time. We hold the unchanging Gospel in one hand and the tools of our time in the other. We worship the Truth. We do not idolize the tools. But we don't neglect them either. We steward both – with reverence for the message and wisdom for the methods.

That's why this conversation matters. Because stewardship requires discernment. It requires you to pay attention not only to what is possible, but to what is wise, loving, and Spirit-led.

And here's the part that feels a little uncomfortable: this moment is bigger than you and me. The decisions we make today about how we use (or refuse) AI will shape not only our ministries but the people we lead and the culture we create.

This is not about being trendy. It's about being trustworthy.

So how do we move forward from here? How do we lead our churches, our teams, and our own hearts into this next season where AI isn't just an optional add-on, but a force that is reshaping how people live, learn, work, and worship? We start with two truths that are essential to hold in tension:

1. **We do not fear the future.** Fear has never been a good guide for the people of God. The same Spirit that raised Jesus from the dead is alive in you. You don't need to fear what's next. You've been equipped for it.

2. **We do not follow the future blindly.** The tools may change, but the mission does not. We don't chase trends for trend's sake. We use tools to serve people, not replace them. We stay anchored in the Gospel while engaging with the world God has placed us in.

Here's the call:

To lead in this moment is to hold hope and caution together. To innovate without compromising your integrity. To harness new tools without handing over your calling.

It's holy work. And you're right in the middle of it.

The Leadership This Moment Needs

Here's what I know about you: You wouldn't have read this far if you were content to coast. You care deeply about leading well – not just managing ministry but shaping it. Forming it. Allowing God to stretch you so that you can serve the people He's entrusted to you.

And that's exactly what this moment needs. Not just early adopters or tech enthusiasts, but discerning, Spirit-led leaders who know how to carry both conviction and curiosity. AI isn't going away. It's not waiting on the sidelines. It's already reshaping how people think, how they create, how they connect. And whether you feel ready or not, your leadership will determine how your church navigates these waters.

AI can learn patterns, but only you can lead people.

The reality? This is not about learning how to use the latest tool. This is about leading a culture. You're not here just to dabble with AI features or find a shortcut for your inbox (though I'm all for saving a little time). You're here because you're called to shape how your people think about technology. How they steward it. How they stay faithful in the face of innovation that moves faster than comfort allows.

The Church has always needed leaders who could discern what's possible and what's profitable for the soul. Leaders who can say, "This is helpful, but this is holy." Leaders who know when to lean into new opportunities and when to pump the brakes. You are those leaders. Or you wouldn't still be here.

But (and this is important) you don't need to be perfect at it. You don't need to know every nuance of machine learning or keep pace with every update. What your people need most is not your expertise. They need your presence. Your willingness to model curiosity. To ask hard questions. To create space for dialogue. To invite others to explore what faithful innovation looks like together.

AI is not the first challenge or opportunity the Church has faced, and it won't be the last. But this moment is asking something of you. Not to become a tech guru. But to become the kind of leader who can guide your church through complexity with clarity, courage, and compassion.

So, take a breath. You're not behind. You're right where you need to be. And this isn't just about AI. This is about the future of the Church's witness in a digital age.

You Don't Have to Be an Expert

Here's some good news: You don't need to be a tech expert to lead your church into the future. You don't need to decode neural networks, master complex prompts, or have a software engineering background. You don't even need to understand exactly how all the algorithms work (I certainly don't).

What you do need? Three things:

1. Stay curious.
2. Stay honest.
3. Stay Spirit-led.

That's it. You don't need to have every answer. But you do need to stay in the conversation.

And before you assume this is going to wreck your budget, take a deep breath. I spend around $100 a month on AI tools. That covers a handful of platforms that help me do everything from summarizing parent interviews to creating training videos, translating communication into multiple languages, supporting graphic design needs, and generating content for our volunteers. That $100 gives me back hours of time, expands my creative bandwidth, and frees me to pour more energy into the people God has entrusted to me.

Could I spend more? Sure. There are enterprise-level AI platforms that cost thousands of dollars. But that's not what this book is about. This book is about equipping local church leaders – Kids Pastors, Worship Directors, Communications Teams, Volunteers, Senior Pastors – faithful people in real ministry settings, doing the good and messy work of loving people well.

And with a few free or low-cost tools, a spirit of curiosity, and the guidance of the Holy Spirit, you can make a real difference. You don't need to be Silicon Valley. You just need to be present. Faithful. Willing.

Not sure where to begin? I've got you. In **Appendix C**, you'll find the exact tools I use along with some beginner-friendly options. These are the platforms I've tested in the trenches of ministry. They're accessible, affordable, and designed to help you build confidence without blowing your budget.

And if you're feeling unsure about the whole "AI literacy" thing, that's okay too. AI literacy isn't about being the smartest person in the room – it's about being a trustworthy one. It's about naming what you know, admitting what you don't, and staying open to learning. When your team sees that you're not pretending to have all the answers, (but you're also not afraid of the questions) they'll follow your lead.

Want to grow your literacy at your own pace? **Appendix D** has a curated list of books, articles, videos, and ministries already modeling what this can look like. Think of it like your AI toolbox. Use what you need, skip what you don't, and keep growing as you go. The goal isn't perfection…it's progress.

The Heart That Drives the Innovation

At the center of all this talk about AI, tools, prompts, and productivity, let's remember the real reason you've stuck with this journey: it's about people. It's about the mission. This conversation isn't just about getting more done or keeping up with the latest trend. It's not even primarily about efficiency (though yes, these tools will save you time). It's about stewardship. It's about leveraging what's available to us today to keep pointing people toward what never changes: Jesus is Lord, and He is not threatened by innovation.

If we're honest, innovation can sometimes feel like a distraction in ministry...like a shiny object or a risky gamble. But I've found that when AI is used well, it doesn't pull me away from my calling. *It pushes me deeper into it.* It clears space. It creates margin. It sparks fresh ideas. It gives me words I couldn't quite find on my own. Sometimes it feels like offering up my loaves and fishes – simple, small, even insufficient – and watching God multiply it into something more.

Not because the tool is magical. But because it's practical. It removes the friction that often slows us down from doing the real, human, Spirit-led work of ministry.

And that's why this chapter isn't just a conclusion. It's a commissioning. You're not just closing the back cover of this book. You're stepping into a new season of leadership.

Your Call as a Ministry Innovator

There's a scene in *Moneyball* (yes, the baseball movie) that captures this spirit perfectly. The front office of the Oakland A's is wrestling with whether to adapt their approach or stick with the "way things have always been done." The GM looks across the room and says plainly: **"adapt or die."**

Now, that's dramatic – but the point holds. The world is shifting. Technology is reshaping how people communicate, learn, work, and yes, even worship. The Church doesn't have to fear that shift. But it does have to face it. And if you've made it this far, I'm guessing you're the kind of leader who sees what's possible before others do. You're a little restless. A little curious. A little tired of hearing, "That's not how we've always done it." And thank God for that.

But just in case you're not quite convinced yet (and at the risk of driving this point home like I'm wielding Thor's hammer at a delicate tea party), let's talk about some innovators and famous missed moments:

- **Wayne Gretzky,** the greatest hockey player of all time, once said, "I skate to where the puck is going to be, not where it has been." That's visionary leadership. We're not called to chase where the world was, we're called to anticipate where God is leading next.

- **Blockbuster and Netflix.** Blockbuster had the chance to buy Netflix for $50 million in the early 2000s. They laughed. Netflix leaned into the future. Blockbuster leaned into nostalgia. One of them adapted. The other... well, there's one lonely Blockbuster left in Bend, Oregon.

- **Kodak and the digital camera.** Kodak actually invented the first digital camera in 1975. But they shelved it, afraid it would cannibalize their film sales. They didn't lose because they lacked innovation. They lost because they feared it.

- **Henry Ford** famously quipped, "If I had asked people what they wanted, they would have said faster horses." (Debatable, but the point stands.) Sometimes leadership isn't about giving people what they know they want, it's about guiding them toward what they need next.

- **Apple and the iPhone.** Before 2007, most people weren't asking for a touchscreen device that combined a phone, camera, and internet browser. Apple anticipated what people didn't know they needed yet. Now? Many of us can't imagine life without one.

- **The Encyclopedia Britannica and Wikipedia.** Britannica ruled for centuries. But when Wikipedia opened the door to crowd-sourced knowledge, Britannica resisted going digital.

Now, Wikipedia has over 6 million English-language articles, and Britannica? It stopped its print editions in 2012.

- **Taxi industry vs. Uber.** Traditional taxi companies operated the same way for decades. Uber entered the scene by leveraging technology, not new cars. They reimagined access, convenience, and customer experience – things the taxi industry hadn't prioritized.

This isn't about chasing trends for trend's sake. It's about being wise stewards of the tools that can help us reach people where they are and where they're going.

Even Jesus had something to say about adapting methods: "No one pours new wine into old wineskins. Otherwise, the new wine will burst the skins; the wine will run out and the wineskins will be ruined. No, new wine must be poured into new wineskins." (Luke 5:37-38)

The Gospel is the wine. It doesn't change. But the wineskins – the methods, the tools, the strategies – they need to stretch with the times.

And that's where you come in. The Church needs leaders like you: leaders who will meet this moment not with fear or arrogance, but with humility, courage, and a willingness to learn.

We don't need more trend-chasers. We need thoughtful, faithful innovators. Leaders who will:

- Ask hard questions. Not just "Can we?" but "Should we?" Not only "What's possible?" but "What's faithful?"
- Build ethical guardrails. Protect what's sacred. Ensure that the tools serve the mission, not the other way around.
- Push for excellence. Don't settle for "good enough." Use these tools to sharpen your communication, clarify your vision, and reach people with creativity and care.
- Champion accessibility. Make sure technology becomes a bridge, not a barrier. Use AI to reach people across languages, learning styles, and platforms.
- Keep the Gospel at the center. Always. The mission isn't to become tech-savvy. The mission is to make disciples.

And here's the best part: You don't need a fancy title to do this. You don't need a vote of approval from every board member. You don't need to launch an initiative or wait for a budget line. You just need conviction. You just need to care.

Because when you lead from that place – when you stay anchored in the Gospel while embracing the tools of our time – you help the Church flourish, not just function. You help it become more agile. More attentive. More invitational. More equipped to meet people where they are.

So here's your charge:

Don't bury your curiosity. Steward it.
Don't downplay your vision. Share it.
Don't wait until every single person is on board.
Start small. Start faithfully.
And let your integrity build the bridge that others will walk across.

Because the future of the Church is not about technology. It's about trust. It's about the people of God, filled with the Spirit of God, using the tools of the time to point to the One who never changes.

When You're Not Sure What to Do Next

Real talk: there will be days when this still feels like too much. When the headlines are louder than your confidence. When the technology outpaces your understanding. When the sheer pace of change makes you want to grab a flip phone, move to the mountains, and start a goat farm.

That's okay. You weren't called to be the expert in everything. You were called to be faithful with what's in your hands. And when the road ahead feels foggy, here are four questions to guide you:

1. **Will this help me love people better?** If it creates more space for relationship, for connection, for meeting people where they are, that's a good sign.

2. **Will this free me to do the work only I can do?** If it handles the grunt work so you can focus on shepherding souls, investing in people, and leading with presence, that's worth it.

3. **Am I using this transparently and ethically?** If you're clear about what you're doing and why, if you're never hiding behind the tool but using it openly, that builds trust.

4. **Have I prayed about this?** No tool, no trend, no technology gets a free pass on that one. Invite the Holy Spirit into the process. Let your prompting start with prayer.

If the answer is yes to these? Then take a step. Not a leap. Not a sprint. Just one faithful step forward.

This book was never meant to be the final word. It's not a manifesto. It's a conversation starter. A flashlight, not a map. The tools will evolve. The debates will shift. There will always be a new app, a new feature, a new headline. But one thing won't change: your calling to lead, to disciple, to love.

When in doubt, don't chase the noise. Return to the mission. Return to the people. Return to the One who called you in the first place.

A Final Word

You don't have to lead the Church of tomorrow with the strategies of yesterday. The world has changed. The mission hasn't. And you, leader, have permission to innovate. Permission to stretch, to experiment, to risk. Permission even to fail (forward).

But here's what matters most: You don't have to do this alone. You have the Holy Spirit. Don't miss that part.

As you explore these tools, as you wrestle with what's wise and what's worth it, as you navigate both skepticism and curiosity in your team meetings, invite God in. Ask Him to lead, to guard, to guide. He's not surprised by AI. He's not pacing the halls of heaven, worried about chatbots and algorithms. And He's certainly not done using you.

This is the God who parted seas with a staff. Who tore down walls with a trumpet blast. Who used a teenage shepherd, a widow's oil, a manger, and a Roman cross. He can absolutely work through your laptop.

So take a breath. Take a step. Take the risk. Because the future of the Church doesn't belong to the fearful. It belongs to the faithful.

And if you ever feel stuck, overwhelmed, or unsure where to begin, remember this: I literally asked an AI tool how to end this book.

It suggested I say: "May your leadership be powered by love, your prompts be effective, and your Wi-Fi signal strong."

Honestly? Not bad. But I think I'll go with this:

May your leadership be powered by the Spirit,
your curiosity fueled by courage,
and your mission always anchored in the hope of Jesus.

So take a deep breath. Open your heart. And step into this new season with courage. This is where the prompt ends. And where faithful practice takes over.

ACKNOWLEDGEMENTS

Turns out writing a book requires more than good ideas and a keyboard; it takes late nights, patient loved ones, and the occasional pep talk (sometimes from actual humans, sometimes from ChatGPT). I'm thankful for the many people who helped carry this across the finish line.

First, thank you to **Ryan and Beth Frank** and the entire **KidzMatter team**. Your unwavering commitment to equipping ministry leaders (especially those serving in the trenches of Kids Ministry) is changing lives and eternities. Thank you for taking a chance on a slightly nerdy, but hopefully deeply needed, book. Your passion for empowering the next generation is contagious, and your belief in this project gave it wings. To Nicole and the publishing team: thank you for walking alongside me through the details, the deadlines, and the "Did I format this correctly?" moments. I'm grateful for your guidance and for your grace.

To **Emily**, thank you for sacrificing time, routines, and many of your quiet hours so that I could get this message on paper. Your support means everything. Thank you for shouldering the chaos of our household with joy, and for cheering me on every step of the way. You embody grace, selflessness, and faithfulness in ways I'll never stop learning from.

To **Hadley, Laikyn, Austyn, Saylor, Waverly, and Brady**, you six are the best part of every day. You are my greatest source of joy, laughter, and inspiration. Your purity, curiosity, and wide-eyed enthusiasm for life challenge me daily to become a better person. I look up to you more than you know. Getting to be your dad is the absolute honor of my life.

More than any sermon I'll ever preach, any book I'll ever write, or any ministry moment I'll ever experience - I hope my life shows you, every single day, that nothing matters more to me than you.

To **Kristen Dalton**, thank you for being a tireless champion of Gospel-centered writing and for bringing both generosity and theological precision to every edit, brainstorm, and conversation. You've sharpened my thinking and reminded me often that communicating the Word of God is both a privilege and a stewardship. Your passion for biblical literacy and discipleship in the way of Jesus has left its mark all over this book and all over my ministry.

To **Tim Thompson**, thank you for inviting me into vocational ministry in the first place. Without your presence in my life, I wouldn't be here writing these words. You were the first to really see something in me - and then call it out. Your belief in my leadership potential, your love for people, and your commitment to keeping the Gospel at the center of everything you do have shaped me in ways that are hard to articulate. You taught me about the ministry of presence before I even knew that phrase existed, and I'll never stop being grateful for your impact on my life and calling.

To **Jordan Jones**, thank you for believing in my voice long before this book existed. Your coaching, encouragement, and freedom to lead have shaped the way I teach, train, and write. You helped me discover how to steward content for actual transformation, not just information. Much of my ability to speak and lead others through innovation started in spaces you created.

And finally, to **you**: the reader. If you've made it this far, you are clearly a growth-minded leader who isn't afraid to ask hard questions or try something new for the sake of the Gospel. Whether we've crossed paths in a breakout room, a leadership session, or a lobby conversation…thank you. Your questions, insights, and curiosity helped shape this book more than you know. I'm praying this book meets you in a moment of holy discontent and moves you forward with courage.

Let's go make something Kingdom-worthy together.

APPENDIX A: ETHICAL GUIDELINES FOR AI USE IN MINISTRY

As ministry leaders, we are called to shepherd people with integrity, humility, and love. AI can be a powerful tool to support that mission, but it must never compromise the Gospel, violate trust, or replace the relational heart of ministry. These ethical guidelines offer a foundation for using AI tools wisely and faithfully:

1. **Prioritize People Over Productivity.** AI should never replace human connection. Use it to support your work, not substitute your presence.

2. **Be Transparent.** Always disclose when AI has contributed to a message, communication, or decision-making process, especially in sensitive or pastoral contexts.

3. **Protect Privacy.** Only input sensitive data (personal details, prayer requests, counseling notes) into AI tools when you are certain that data is secure, private, and compliant with local regulations. When in doubt, leave it out.

4. **Check for Bias and Accuracy.** AI models reflect the data they were trained on, which can include biases or inaccuracies. Always review AI-generated content carefully. Don't trust the tool without discernment.

5. **Use AI to Empower, Not Exploit.** AI should expand access, serve diverse needs (like language translation or accessibility), and equip your team. Avoid using it in ways that manipulate or mislead.

6. **Guard Against Over-dependence.** AI can streamline tasks, but don't let it numb your creativity, intuition, or spiritual discernment. Stay connected to your calling, not just your calendar.

7. **Keep the Gospel at the Center.** Use AI to amplify what matters most: the hope of Jesus. If a tool ever clouds that message or compromises your mission, it's time to reevaluate.

Remember: AI is a tool. The Holy Spirit is your guide. Let technology serve your ministry, not steer it.

APPENDIX B: AI INTEGRATION ASSESSMENT FOR CHURCHES

Before adopting AI tools in your church, it's wise to pause, reflect, and assess where you are and where you want to go. This simple assessment will help you gauge your church's readiness for AI integration and highlight areas where you can lead with greater clarity, care, and confidence.

1. Mission Alignment

    a. Does this AI tool help fulfill our church's mission to make disciples and love people well?

    b. Will it support our core values and enhance (not replace) relational ministry?

Assessment:
- ☐ Fully aligned
- ☐ Somewhat aligned (needs discussion)
- ☐ Not aligned (needs reevaluation)

2. Leadership Readiness

    a. Are key leaders informed and engaged in the conversation about AI adoption?

    b. Do we have a clear, shared vision for why and how we are integrating AI?

Assessment:

- ❑ Fully ready
- ❑ Somewhat ready (needs further dialogue)
- ❑ Not ready (needs leadership development)

3. Team and Volunteer Readiness

    a. How comfortable is our team with technology in general?

    b. Have we addressed common fears or misconceptions about AI with education and transparency?

Assessment:

- ❑ Highly comfortable and informed
- ❑ Somewhat comfortable (needs training)
- ❑ Uncomfortable (needs significant onboarding)

4. Ethical Safeguards

    a. Do we have ethical guidelines in place for how AI will be used in our ministry (see Appendix A)?

    b. Are we transparent with our congregation about when and how AI tools are used?

Assessment:

- ❑ Guidelines established and practiced
- ❑ Some guidelines in place (needs refinement)
- ❑ No guidelines (needs immediate attention)

5. Data Privacy and Security
    a. Do we understand the privacy policies of the AI tools we're using?

    b. Are we cautious with sensitive data (e.g., personal info, prayer requests)?

Assessment:
- ☐ Strong data practices in place
- ☐ Some awareness (needs review)
- ☐ No clear practices (needs urgent action)

6. Financial Stewardship
    a. Are we investing in AI tools that align with our budget and ministry priorities?

    b. Are we making use of free or low-cost tools before investing in premium platforms?

Assessment:
- ☐ Fully aligned with budget and stewardship goals
- ☐ Needs adjustment (exploring options)
- ☐ Misaligned (needs reevaluation)

7. Spiritual Discernment
    a. Have we prayed and sought wise counsel about AI adoption in our ministry?

    b. Are we inviting the Holy Spirit to guide our decisions and use of these tools?

Assessment:
- ☐ Actively practicing discernment
- ☐ Somewhat practicing (needs more intentionality)
- ☐ Not practicing (needs immediate focus)

Reflection Questions:

1. Where are we strong?
2. Where do we need to grow?
3. What is one next faithful step we can take toward wise AI integration?

Tip: Revisit this assessment regularly (at least annually) as technology evolves and your ministry context shifts.

APPENDIX C: RECOMMENDED RESOURCES TO DEVELOP AI LITERACY

Disclaimer: These resources offer valuable insights into artificial intelligence. While I've personally found them helpful, I don't necessarily endorse every view expressed by their authors. Approach with discernment and an open heart.

Books on AI

Theological and Christian Perspectives:

1. *The Age of AI: Artificial Intelligence and the Future of Humanity* by Jason Thacker. A thoughtful exploration of AI's implications for Christian ethics and society

2. *God, Human, Animal, Machine: Technology, Metaphor, and the Search for Meaning* by Meghan O'Gieblyn. Written by a former believer, this book wrestles with the spiritual questions AI raises for all of us.

3. *Teaching with AI: A Practical Guide to a New Era of Human Learning* by José Antonio Bowen & C. Edward Watson: While not explicitly Christian, this practical guide offers applicable wisdom for ministry leaders navigating AI.

Secular Books (Theory, Ethics, and Application):

1. *Superintelligence* by Nick Bostrom. A philosophical exploration of AI's future and the risks of advanced machine intelligence.

2. *Life 3.0: Being Human in the Age of Artificial Intelligence* by Max Tegmark. A look at how AI could shape the future of life on Earth (and beyond).
3. *Artificial Intelligence: A Guide for Thinking Humans* by Melanie Mitchell. An accessible, practical overview of AI's current state and limitations.
4. *Weapons of Math Destruction* by Cathy O'Neil. A sobering look at the ethical risks and societal impacts of algorithmic decision-making.
5. *AI Ethics* by Mark Coeckelbergh. A comprehensive review of the moral questions surrounding AI development.

Digital Articles, Blogs, and Organizations

1. Carey Nieuwhof: The Ultimate Guide to AI, Pastors, and the Church. A practical introduction to AI in ministry from one of today's most influential church leadership voices. https://careynieuwhof.com/the-ultimate-guide-to-a-i-pastors-and-the-church/
2. AI for Church Leaders. A growing hub of resources on how church leaders can wisely use AI tools. https://www.aiforchurchleaders.com/
3. Gloo: AI & the Church. Research and resources at the intersection of data, technology, and ministry. https://gloo.com/ai
4. AI and Faith. An organization exploring the relationship between artificial intelligence and religious beliefs. https://aiandfaith.org/
5. OpenAI News. Stay informed about the latest developments in AI technology. https://openai.com/news/

Podcasts

1. Carey Nieuwhof Leadership Podcast: AI Miniseries. Essential listening for ministry leaders navigating AI. Key episodes include:
   a. Episode 605: John Wyatt on breakthroughs in AI and the need for theological voices.

b. Episode 606: John Lennox on Revelation, AI threats, and human agency.

c. Episode 607: Ann Skeet & Brian Green on trust crises and ethical gaps in AI.

d. Episode 608: Kenny Jahng on church tech stacks and the upside/downside of AI.

Online Courses and Tutorials

1. RightNow Media: Ministry in the Age of AI. A faith-based introduction to AI's role in church leadership and discipleship. https://www.rightnowmedia.org/webinar/ministry-in-the-age-of-ai

2. Coursera: AI for Everyone by Andrew Ng. An excellent beginner course for understanding the basics of AI and its implications across industries. https://www.coursera.org/specializations/machine-learning-introduction

3. edX: Artificial Intelligence by Principles and Techniques. A deeper dive for those interested in understanding the technical side of AI. https://www.edx.org/learn/computer-programming/raspberry-pi-foundation-introduction-to-machine-learning-and-ai

Webinars and Conferences

1. AI for Church Leaders (Workshops). Regularly hosted practical workshops equipping ministry leaders to explore AI in their contexts. https://www.aiforchurchleaders.com/next

2. AI and Faith Summit. An annual conference focused on ethical and theological engagement with AI. https://aiandfaith.org/external-events/

3. Barna Webinar: Ministry in the Age of AI. A discussion of Barna's latest research and best practices for ministry leaders in this new technological landscape. https://www.barna.com/webinars/ministry-in-the-age-of-ai/

Suggested Next Steps

1. Pick **one book** (Christian or secular) to read in the next three months.
2. Listen to **one podcast episode** on AI and ministry leadership.
3. Explore **one free course** to strengthen your AI literacy.

The goal isn't to become an expert overnight. The goal is to grow, stay curious, and lead with wisdom.

APPENDIX D: RECOMMENDED TOOLS FOR AN AI-POWERED MINISTRY

Disclaimer: While these resources offer valuable applications of AI, I do not necessarily endorse or agree with all the views expressed by their creators. Please use discernment and evaluate each tool through the lens of your ministry's values, theology, and privacy standards.

Chatbots & Large Language Models (LLMs)

For brainstorming, writing drafts, summarizing, and more.

1. ChatGPT (by OpenAI)
2. Claude (by Anthropic)
3. Gemini (by Google)
4. Llama (by Meta)
5. Grok (by xAI)
6. Pi (by Inflection)
7. Searchie (designed for content creators to build searchable libraries and automate responses)

Virtual Assistants & Copilots

For daily productivity, task automation, and assistance.

1. Copilot (by Microsoft)
2. Jasper (focused on marketing content creation)
3. Jarvis (alternative virtual assistant platform)
4. Siri, Alexa, Google Assistant (general-purpose virtual assistants)

Graphic Design & Video Editing

For creating visual content, sermon graphics, volunteer training materials, and social media posts.

1. Canva (user-friendly design platform with AI-powered tools)
2. DALL-E (by OpenAI; AI-generated imagery)
3. Midjourney (advanced AI art generation)
4. Stable Diffusion (open-source AI art generator)
5. Adobe Spark (easy-to-use design platform)
6. Animoto (video creation tool for social media and presentations)
7. HeyGen (AI-powered video translation, realistic avatars, and lip-syncing – ideal for multilingual training or outreach videos)

Writing & Speaking

For generating content, refining sermons, and improving communication.

1. Writesonic (content generation with templates for various needs)
2. Rytr (affordable AI writing assistant)
3. Yoodli (free AI-powered communication coach that analyzes your speaking habits, filler words, pacing, and tone – perfect for sermon prep and leadership development)

Meeting Notes & Speech-to-Text

For recording, transcribing, summarizing, and analyzing meetings or sermons.

1. Otter (real-time transcription and summarization)
2. Read AI (meeting summarization and action items)
3. Fireflies (meeting assistant that records and analyzes conversations)

Voice Cloning & Audio Production

For creating multilingual videos, voiceovers, or unique audio content.

1. Murf (AI voice generator and text-to-speech platform)
2. ElevenLabs (advanced voice cloning and synthesis)
3. Suno (AI-powered songwriting and music production tool; capable of generating full-length, radio-quality songs from text prompts)

Research & Knowledge Discovery

For summarizing research articles, compiling insights, and assisting in theological or cultural studies.

1. Consensus (AI-powered search engine for academic research)
2. Quivr (AI assistant for organizing and recalling knowledge)

Mentorship & Connection Building

For developing coaching, discipleship, and mentoring relationships within your ministry.

1. MentorcliQ (mentorship program management)
2. Mentorly (virtual mentorship platform)

APPENDIX E: EXAMPLE CHATGPT PROMPTS FOR MINISTRY LEADERS

How to Craft Effective Prompts Using Task, Format, Voice, and Context

Great prompting is an art form. When you combine clarity with creativity, AI becomes a powerful ministry partner. The prompts below follow the **Four Elements of a Great Prompt** framework introduced in this book:

1. **Task** – What you want the AI to do
2. **Format** – The output style you want (list, paragraph, outline, etc.)
3. **Voice** – The tone or personality (pastoral, energetic, formal, conversational)
4. **Context** – The background or specifics to make the prompt relevant

Use these examples as templates for your own leadership, communication, and creativity.

1. **Sermon Preparation and Brainstorming**
   a. "Brainstorm 10 sermon illustration ideas about perseverance, drawing from both modern life examples and biblical stories. Provide them as a bullet-point list, with a pastoral and hopeful tone. I'm preaching to a multi-generational church in a suburban setting."

b. "Summarize key themes from the Gospel of John in a way that's accessible for a congregation unfamiliar with theological jargon. Use a warm, conversational voice and format as a teaching outline for a sermon series."

2. **Event Planning and Creative Ideas**

a. "Generate 5 creative outreach event ideas for a mid-sized church in the Midwest aiming to connect with young families. Include seasonal themes for spring or summer, and present them as a bullet-point list with a brief description for each."

b. "Provide a 2-minute opening prayer for a volunteer training event that feels inspiring but practical. Use a tone that acknowledges the importance of volunteers in kids and youth ministry."

3. **Volunteer Communication and Training**

a. "Draft a one-page welcome letter for new volunteers in the hospitality ministry. Use a warm, encouraging tone and include a bullet-point list of key expectations and a short paragraph about the mission of hospitality at our church."

b. "Create a training handout on conflict resolution for small group leaders. Use a clear, step-by-step format, include scripture references, and maintain a pastoral but practical voice."

4. **Parent Communication and Engagement**

a. "Write a follow-up email for parents after a kids ministry event, summarizing what their children learned about prayer. Use a friendly, conversational voice and include 3 suggestions for parents to reinforce the lesson at home."

b. "Suggest 5 creative ways for parents to foster gratitude in their children at home during the Thanksgiving season. Provide as a bullet-point list with simple, practical activities, and use a family-friendly, encouraging tone."

5. **Content Analysis and Strategy**

   a. "Analyze the following transcript of our staff brainstorming session on improving worship services [insert transcript]. Summarize key themes and suggest next steps. Use a concise, bullet-point summary format with a collaborative, solution-focused tone."

   b. "Review this draft of our church mission statement [insert statement]. Provide 3 suggestions to make it more memorable and engaging for first-time guests. Use a clear, encouraging voice and format as a bullet-point list."

6. **Behavior Management and Volunteer Support**

   a. "Create a guide for volunteers on trauma-informed behavior management techniques for kids ministry. Include 5 best practices, formatted as a list with brief explanations, and maintain a supportive, confident tone."

   b. "List 5 strategies to help volunteers stay motivated and engaged over a busy ministry season. Include practical tips and use a conversational, uplifting tone."

7. **Spiritual Formation and Discipleship Tools**

   a. "Develop a Bible reading plan for small groups focusing on spiritual resilience. Include a 6-week schedule with key scriptures and a reflection question for each week. Use a pastoral tone and format it as an easy-to-follow outline."

   b. "Generate 5 creative prayer station ideas for a Good Friday service. Ensure they are reflective, interactive, and suitable for all ages. Present them as a numbered list with brief descriptions."

8. **Strategic Planning and Feedback**
    a. "Create a SWOT analysis (Strengths, Weaknesses, Opportunities, Threats) for our church's online ministry presence. Use the following data as context: [insert web traffic data, social engagement, etc.]. Format as a 4-column table with bullet points."
    b. "Summarize the results of our recent church-wide survey [insert results]. Identify top concerns and opportunities for growth, and suggest 3 potential initiatives. Use a concise tone and format as a bulleted list."

9. **Translating and Adapting Content**
    a. "Translate this ministry training outline into Spanish [insert outline]. Ensure the tone remains warm and inviting, suitable for volunteers with varying levels of formal education."
    b. "Adapt this devotional about forgiveness [insert content] for a youth group audience. Use a more casual, relatable tone and format it as a 5-minute teaching script."

These prompts aren't the limit, they're the launchpad. Customize them. Play with them. Let them reflect your voice, your context, and your ministry's unique needs.

For more tips on crafting great prompts, **revisit Chapter 7: The Power of Prompt Engineering** in this book.

APPENDIX F: FAQS ABOUT AI AND THE CHURCH

Is AI really necessary for ministry?

AI isn't necessary the way prayer, Scripture, or community is. But it's useful…the same way microphones, church databases, or livestreams became useful. It helps remove friction, freeing you up to focus on what only you can do: be fully present with people. AI is simply a tool – one that, if stewarded wisely, can amplify your mission without replacing your calling.

Will AI replace pastors, teachers, or worship leaders?

Nope. Not even close. AI can write outlines, suggest creative ideas, or automate some admin work, but it can't lay hands on the sick, offer pastoral presence, or discern the Spirit's leading in a room. Ministry is relational, Spirit-filled work. AI can serve it, but it can never substitute for it.

Isn't using AI in church "cheating"?

Is using a microwave cheating at cooking? Is using spell-check cheating at writing? AI is just a modern tool for efficiency and creativity. It helps get you 60% of the way there so you can focus on refining, discerning, and personalizing. With ethical use, it's not cheating, it's collaborating.

How can I be sure AI isn't producing biased or inaccurate content?

You can't blindly trust AI. That's why discernment matters. AI reflects the data it's trained on, which means it can carry cultural, theological, or systemic biases. Always check AI outputs against Scripture, theology, and your community's context. Use it as a conversation starter, not a final authority.

Is AI safe to use with sensitive church data?

Not all AI tools are created equal when it comes to data privacy. Be sure to review a tool's privacy policies and avoid inputting sensitive personal data (like prayer requests or confidential counseling notes) into general-purpose platforms. Use AI for drafts, summaries, or public-facing content, but keep private pastoral work, well, private.

How much should I budget for AI tools?

Surprisingly little! You don't need a Silicon Valley budget to get started. I spend about $100/month on a variety of AI tools that help with communication, translation, training materials, songwriting, and more. Many tools offer free plans or low-cost tiers, so you can experiment without breaking the bank. (Check out **Appendix C** for specific recommendations!)

Isn't this just a passing trend? Will I waste time learning AI?

AI is not a fad. It's as embedded in modern life as email or social media. Even if the specific tools change, the core technology – machine learning, automation, and content generation – is here to stay. Investing in AI literacy now will help you stay nimble as the landscape evolves.

How do I introduce AI to a skeptical church team?

Start with transparency and small wins. Don't hide that you're using AI. Explain how it's serving your team (like summarizing parent feedback or creating training materials in multiple languages). Share examples that are personal and mission-focused. (For more on leading change, revisit **Chapter 9**!)

How do I make sure I'm using AI ethically?

Stay grounded in your mission. Keep asking:

1. Does this uphold dignity and truth?
2. Am I using this tool transparently?
3. Is this freeing me up for deeper relational ministry?

Check out **Appendix A: Ethical Guidelines for AI Use in Ministry** for practical steps.

What if I feel overwhelmed and don't know where to start?

You're not alone! Start small. Pick one task that feels repetitive or draining (a volunteer email, a sermon brainstorm, a feedback summary), and experiment with AI there. You don't need to be an expert. You just need to be curious. (And don't miss **Appendix D: Recommended Resources to Develop AI Literacy** to grow at your own pace.)

APPENDIX G: GLOSSARY OF AI TERMS FOR MINISTRY LEADERS

Terms listed in conceptual order. For quick reference, see alphabetical index at the end.

Artificial Intelligence (AI)

Any technology that mimics human behavior, decision-making, or learning. In other words: it's not a person, but it acts like one in specific ways – making decisions, learning patterns, or responding to input. AI can range from chatbots that answer FAQs to tools that write content, translate languages, or recommend songs.

Machine Learning (ML)

A type of AI where computers "learn" from data and get better over time without being explicitly programmed for every task. Think of it like a toddler with flashcards: show it enough examples (cats, dogs, pizza), and eventually it starts recognizing patterns (like that pizza isn't a dog… though that might depend on your toddler).

Deep Learning

A more advanced form of machine learning that uses layered structures called neural networks – inspired by how the human brain works – to recognize complex patterns. If machine learning is a toddler with flash-cards, deep learning is that same toddler who's just discovered espresso.

Neural Network

The system of interconnected nodes that deep learning uses to process information. Picture it like a massive web of "neurons" (inspired by your brain), where data travels through different layers to make decisions or predictions. (But no, it doesn't have a soul or even a favorite Bible verse.)

Narrow AI (Artificial Narrow Intelligence, ANI)

AI that's designed to be really good at one thing - like playing chess, recognizing faces, or transcribing sermons. Your Spotify recommendations? Narrow AI. The tool helping you draft emails? Narrow AI. It's smart, but only in its lane.

General AI (Artificial General Intelligence, AGI)

This is the stuff of science fiction (for now). AGI would be an AI system that can understand, learn, and apply knowledge across a wide range of tasks, much like a human. Picture a robot that could lead worship, preach a sermon, fix the soundboard, and still remember to order donuts for guest services. We're not there (yet).

Superintelligence (Artificial Superintelligence, ASI)

The hypothetical stage where AI surpasses human intelligence in every area: creativity, wisdom, problem-solving, emotional intelligence, and beyond. It's like the big boss level of AI. Don't worry: this is purely theoretical at this point. Your church coffee machine is not plotting to out-preach you.

Large Language Model (LLM)

A type of AI trained on massive amounts of text data to generate human-like language responses. ChatGPT is one example. These models can summarize, translate, brainstorm, or generate content based on the input you give them (called prompts). Think of it like a supercharged conversation partner (without the need for caffeine).

Prompt Engineering

The art of crafting clear, specific instructions (prompts) to get the best results from AI tools like ChatGPT. In this book, we introduced **The Four Elements of a Great Prompt**:

1. Task (What do you want it to do?)
2. Format (What kind of output do you want?)
3. Voice (What tone or style do you want?)
4. Context (What background or details should it consider?)

If you ask vague questions, you get vague answers. If you ask great questions, you unlock great responses. Prompt engineering is learning how to ask well.

Chatbot

A software application that mimics human conversation (usually via text) answering questions or guiding users through processes. Think of it like an automated greeter or FAQ specialist. Some are basic (yes/no answers). Others (like ChatGPT) are highly advanced, able to write sermons, brainstorm VBS themes, or offer pastoral prompts (though they still can't visit someone in the hospital).

Bias (in AI)

When AI systems produce results that unfairly favor or disfavor certain groups, ideas, or perspectives – often unintentionally – because of the data they were trained on. For example: If a language model was trained mostly on Western sources, it may not understand global church contexts as well. This is why human oversight and discernment are essential.

Algorithm

A set of rules or instructions AI follows to process data and produce results. In ministry terms: it's like your VBS volunteer sign-up process – step--by-step logic, but with fewer last-minute cancellations.

Automation

The use of technology to perform tasks without human intervention. In churches, automation could mean automatically sending follow-up emails to new guests or scheduling social media posts. AI takes this a step further by allowing for personalized, dynamic automation (like customizing messages based on user behavior).

Data Privacy

The practice of ensuring that personal information (like names, emails, prayer requests) is handled securely and ethically, especially when AI tools are involved. In ministry, this means making sure any data you use or share (especially with AI tools) respects confidentiality and aligns with your church's privacy policies.

API (Application Programming Interface)

A system that allows different software programs to communicate and work together.

Think of it like the translator between your church database and your online giving platform – or between your sermon library and an AI tool that helps repurpose your content.

Generative AI

AI that creates new content (like text, images, music, or video) based on the data it has been trained on. Examples include ChatGPT (text), DALL-E (images), Suno (music), and HeyGen (videos). In ministry, this could mean creating sermon graphics, generating volunteer training videos, or writing a new worship song (just maybe don't let AI name your next worship album – unless you want "Hallelujah 3000").

Feel free to revisit this glossary anytime your brain starts spinning in the AI whirlwind. And remember: You don't need to master every term. You just need enough to lead with confidence, curiosity, and discernment.

APPENDIX H: ALPHABETICAL INDEX OF AI TERMS FOR MINISTRY LEADERS

www.ingramcontent.com/pod-product-compliance
Lightning Source LLC
Chambersburg PA
CBHW071151120626
46546CB00006B/2214